LOW FLYING HEROES

Micro-social enterprise below the radar screen

Alex MacGillivray, Pat Conaty
and Chris Wadhams

CONTENTS

EXECUTIVE SUMMARY

The 'radar screen' which measures activity in the voluntary sector is fine for tracking the movements of large organisations that move sluggishly though society. The screen is now being tuned to pick up the glittering trajectory of the occasional social entrepreneur. But this report shows that our radar screen is failing to pick up huge numbers of small, dynamic, informal groups in Britain's 20,000 communities. The failure to understand and support micro-social enterprise is a considerable missed opportunity. But corrective action could for once be quite easy.

This report shows that there are many more groups than most policy-makers realise, and that they are highly effective. There are now too many 'pilot' schemes trying to support them, but not enough scaled-up resources to meet the potential demand of hundreds of thousands of groups.

There has been admirable talk and a comprehensive process leading to a national strategy for neighbourhood renewal. There has been a recent proliferation of grant schemes (over 50 at last count). Yet the needs and potential of these groups are little understood.

Our in-depth profiles from Hastings and Birmingham show them to be quick-witted and flexible enough to be making real progress in tackling poverty, renewing neighbourhoods, building social capital, economic inclusion and making communities green and sustainable. Meanwhile, despite a high premium placed on 'partnership', larger, more traditional, outside agencies often privately admit they are floundering.

Neither mini-charities nor micro-businesses, the 'low flying heroes' are highly informal outfits that defy easy definition. They are an unlikely blend of Dad's Army and Arthur Daley. They are either invisible or irritating to most funders and policy makers, hence the label conveying their sense of embattled and even surreptitious purpose. They are flying below the 'official' radar screen. The label is certainly not intended to imply gender. Many, perhaps most, are women. Nor are we suggesting that their skill in ducking and diving through red tape is anything other than legal.

There is an increasingly sterile debate between advocates of social entrepreneurs and those who support group-based community activism. To side-step this debate, we have reluctantly coined a new name for the low flying heroes: 'micro-social enterprises' (and so apologies for yet another acronym, the MSE). They are small, energetic, informal outfits operating at community level, motivated by social and environmental benefits. Resources of all kinds are tight: an MSE can be defined as a coherent and effective community group that does not have any of the following:

- *staff*: people working full time, with job titles and salaries
- *office*: regular premises, equipment, stationery and business cards
- *funding*: dependable ongoing income of any significance
- *formalities*: legal definitions, registered charity numbers or 'agms'

To make up for this, what the MSE does have is a team of people with a great idea, boundless enthusiasm, and the nous to make things happen.

There are 600–900,000 micro social enterprises in the UK – more than three times as many as the formal charities. Between 1.8 million and 5.4 million people are actively involved in these MSEs. We urgently need a more reliable database at local and regional level, to target support to where it is needed. Inner cities and affluent neighbourhoods may both be relatively densely served – but for different reasons. Outer estates and some rural areas appear to be less so. We need to be able to judge which initiatives are thriving, which struggling and which moribund. And while most are socially inclusive, we need to spot those which are divisive.

This New Economics Foundation report was commissioned by the Joseph Rowntree Foundation and forms part of our long-running programme on community enterprise. The findings are based on detailed interviews carried out with low flying heroes in one industrial city – Birmingham – and a seaside town – Hastings. It has no pretensions of being a statistical sample. The report tells some of their colourful stories in a series of case studies.

The report emphasises that informal community action is incredibly diverse.

Diversity is clear in:

- *motivation and inspiration*, from self-interest to mutuality to selfless altruism. Not many see themselves as heroes, and some probably aren't.

- *group dynamic*, from the charismatic solo entrepreneurs through dynamic duos to team efforts, which are less media friendly – and so less celebrated.

- *gender and ethnicity*: the majority of low flying 'heroes' are probably women, with ethnic and faith communities well represented. Ironically, 'majority' groups like white low-waged males may not be so well served.

- *ambition and development*, from bumping along the bottom quite happily with little or no income to becoming a big player in the 'real' (ie formal) voluntary sector.

- *access to resources*, from groups that could collapse for want of £50 to those that have an uncanny ability to press the right fundraising buttons. But it goes far beyond money: media coverage, training and workspace are also hard to get hold of.

- *relationships*: some groups thrive in adversity (hence the war-like tone of the title low flying heroes). Others need a supportive environment. Despite fine words, support cannot be taken for granted from local and central government, or even from the formal voluntary sector, who sometimes play dirty for a piece of the action.

New support mechanisms must take full account of this diversity. This should be obvious, but alarmingly, many policy-makers and funders have a single vision – sometimes tunnel vision and a one-track mind – about how every group should be constituted, how it should operate and where it should be heading. There is no one-size-fits-all.

It is good news that the Home Office's Active Community Unit and DETR's new Neighbourhood Renewal Unit are beginning to play a leading role in challenging stereotypes and broadening the vision across government and beyond. There are encouraging signs of joined-up thinking, but as yet most of these are at the community level and among senior civil servants. In the middle echelons of central and local government, and in the voluntary sector too, thinking is still highly compartmentalised.

The recent raft of financial support packages – over 50 at last count – are welcome, and will all in all reach some tens of thousands of low flying heroes. But there are serious doubts about whether the coverage of these packages is adequate to the need, and they are beginning to look like a rash of 'initiativitis'. While many local schemes are admirable, there are no mechanisms to ensure that they learn from each other. On past experience, up to half could fail, and there is no guarantee that government will enable the remaining half to evolve into a national system of support for all social entrepreneurs, fully integrated with the benefits regime and lifelong learning.

Even if enough cash is eventually allocated, it has to be given in the right way at the right time. Stepped grants, loans, performance-related funding, streamlined application forms like the Lottery's Awards for All, and long term core support would all be welcome supplements or alternatives to the current concentration on one-off grants. It sounds strange but groups can find it stressful to be given a £2,000 cheque out of the blue that they have to spend fast.

Misplaced concerns over financial accountability have led to a bureaucratic nightmare for some low flying heroes and their intermediaries. Abuses of public funding do not happen in small scale projects where scores of local volunteers act as 'sweat equity watchdogs'. Constraining spending options and drowning community activists in paperwork is counter-productive. Peer group audits between local groups are one cost-effective alternative; a web-based accountability tool is also being promoted for the co-operative movement. Time-based accounting also reveals exactly who is contributing most resources, and so who the group should be accountable to. In many cases, costing volunteers' time at the minimum wage shows that local people have funded the lion's share of a project, and will not tolerate any abuse.

Money is not the only need, nor always the top priority. Low flying heroes also want help with:

- *networking with like-minded people*, in their area and on the other side of the country, through newsletters, electronic networks, reciprocal visits and exchanges. Time banking can help leverage extra resources; 'enterprise coaching' is another promising new approach.

- *practical and innovative advice on how to form an appropriate institution*: the Charity Commission should consider a revised form of charitable status available for ultra-small groups now that community capacity building has been accepted as charitable in low-income areas; and other interesting models should be made available (eg mini-mutuals).

- *opting out of the predominant growth model*, including encouragement to disband (horror of horrors) when a goal is accomplished. There is little evidence in the voluntary sector that a group's effectiveness increases with age, fundraising savvy or number of full-time paid managers.

- *access to appropriate premises and facilities*, such as managed workspaces earmarked for community groups, affordable and convenient premises for meetings, shared internet and web access, call centres. There is a crucial role for dedicated social enterprise zones and incubators, so long as they don't get squeezed out during the next property boom.

- *winning both practical and moral support*, which means tackling the ugly root causes of jealousy, co-option and in-fighting that too often make up the real deal between the powers-that-be and informal groups. Recognition and being valued are very important, so the media has a role to play, too.

- *dealing with well-intentioned as well as petty-minded and obstructive bureaucracy*, including a counter-productive benefits regime and over-zealous interpretation and enforcement in local offices.

- *sometimes, just being left alone to get on with it.*

The final section of the report discusses the pros and cons of these policy recommendations in detail. It concludes that far more tailor-made support should be given to low flying heroes. This is labour intensive but costs can be minimised by funding 'horizontal' support among clusters of low flying heroes rather than top-down and one-on-one relationships. Getting the support right will enable these low flying heroes to continue and even increase their impressive work.

ACKNOWLEDGEMENTS

Our thanks go first and foremost to the many low flying heroes in Birmingham and Hastings, who gave up precious time to tell us their stories. They are named in this report. We are also indebted to the people and organisations making most progress in supporting these and other MSEs, particularly Naomi Alexander, Joan Blaney, Dorothy Newton and Matthew Pike of the Scarman Trust; John Turner and Renate Reuther-Greaves of the Hastings Trust; and Vanessa Cusack of the Quest Trust.

Many thanks for their helpful advice and trenchant criticism to the project's advisory group: Gabriel Chanan, Community Development Foundation; Barry Knight, CENTRIS; Jeremy Kendall, London School of Economics; Doreen Finneron, Church Urban Fund; Simon Bale, Communities Organised for a Greater Bristol; Amanda Paul; Bryn Higgs, Community Catalyst; Rowan Astbury, Charities Evaluation Services; John Roberts and Alan Brown, DETR; Audrey Bronstein, Oxfam; and Claudia Kenyatta, then at the Cabinet Office Social Exclusion Unit's Policy Action Team on Community Self Help. Fred Rattley of the Allens Croft project made helpfully challenging comments, while we also benefited from insights from Judith Hanna, James Smith, Konrad Elsdon, Charles Handy, Parin Moledina, Annabel Jackson, Libby Bradshaw, Andrew Farrow and Hilary Burrage.

Peter Marcus and John Low at the Joseph Rowntree Foundation gave more than just financial support, while Perry Walker, Ed Mayo, Elna Kotze, Peter Ramsden, Sue Carter and Pete Raynard at NEF all helped with ideas and logistics. Leonie Greene deserves special thanks for painting and donating the lovely watercolour painting on the cover of this report. As ever, any mistakes and omissions that have slipped through these nets are the sole responsibility of the authors.

ABOUT NEW ECONOMICS FOUNDATION

The New Economics Foundation (NEF) is one of the UK's most creative and effective independent think tanks. Our mission is to help build a just and sustainable economy with ideas and action that put people and the planet first.

The new economy is here already. It is being built in practice through a wide range of initiatives, from ethical investment to community finance to organic agriculture. These approaches are human in scale, accept and nurture implicit values, believe in sufficiency not growth-for-growth's-sake, and promote social justice and the accountability of organisations to all their stakeholders.

Founded in 1986, NEF works in the UK and internationally with a wide range of partners, and at all levels from the village hall to Whitehall. Most of our projects involve a blend of research, training, education and policy. NEF has 35 staff working from its London office, and thousands of supporters around the country.

NEF is a registered charity (number 1055254), funded in equal proportions by individual supporters, charitable trusts, public grants and business partnerships. NEF's director is Ed Mayo.

Enterprising communities

This report is the latest in NEF's long-running series of reports on community enterprise. The first was *Towards a New Sector: macro-policies for community enterprise* (1992), in which Tim Crabtree and Andy Roberts argued for a new legal status of 'not-for-profit companies'.

Next came *Community Works*, a pocket directory of 34 activities that are being undertaken in communities of all shapes and sizes across the UK, from organic box schemes to credit unions to local bartering. Some 50,000 copies have been distributed since 1997.

This was followed by John Pearce's *Measuring Social Wealth*, a 1997 study showing how social auditing could be put into practice for community and co-operative enterprises, drawing extensively on case studies from Scotland and elsewhere.

In 1998, we published *Practical People, Noble Causes*, a case study based research report by Simon Zadek and Stephen Thake on community-based social entrepreneurs, which identified the need for support, training and above all a guaranteed income for these individuals.

In 1999 came *Micro Credit for Micro Enterprise*, by Pat Conaty and Thomas Fisher, which identified the need for far more flexible funding options for the dynamic micro-business sector in the UK, which could be more dynamic still if its needs had not been studiously ignored for decades in favour of inward investment strategies.

In 2000, we collaborated with IPPR to publish *Micro-Entrepreneurs: creating enterprising communities*, by Andrea Westall, Peter Ramsden and Julie Foley. The case studies in this report demonstrate just how significant is the job-creation potential of small businesses in disadvantaged areas. In October 2001, we will launch a series of Inner City 100 awards for fast growing businesses, supported by the Royal Bank of Scotland Group and HM Treasury. In 2000, we also launched *Charitable Trust*, by Peter Raynard and Sara Murphy; this report is based on social audits of a dozen voluntary organisations and sets a new agenda for accountability in the sector.

For further information about NEF's work on community enterprise, please contact:

Sarah McGeehan
New Economics Foundation,
Cinnamon House, Cole Street, London SE1 4YH, UK
Tel: 020 7407 7447 Fax: 020 7407 6473
Email: info@neweconomics.org Website: www.neweconomics. org

Co-author Chris Wadhams can be reached at 131 Newbridge Road, Birmingham B9 5JF. Tel: 0121 784 3292. Email: cwadhams@hotmail.com

INTRODUCTION

Micro social enterprises: what are they?

This report is about 'micro social enterprises'. This is a new term invented by the authors to define a huge number of small, energetic, informal outfits operating at community level, motivated by social and environmental benefits. Resources of all kinds are usually tight. Perhaps as a result, the work of such groups is innovative, inclusive and disproportionately effective. Community business, local self-help and mutual aid are other terms that capture many aspects of the phenomenon.

On 'sink' estates and in posh suburbs alike, family, next-door neighbours and friends help each other out, and in most of Britain's 20,000 neighbourhoods, there will also be one or more local charities, tenants' associations or other formal groups doing good work. The MSE is an outfit that falls half way between these spontaneous familial and organised charitable forms. A recent report[1] usefully distinguished different types of community and voluntary activity, which help locate the MSEs:

- Family and neighbours (eg 'favours')
- Informal community action (what we call the MSEs)
- Formal community action (eg Neighbourhood Watch; church groups)
- 'Formal' voluntary organisations (eg Charity Shops, local branches)

As a very rough rule of thumb, there could be anywhere between half a dozen and a dozen MSEs in a typical community of 3,000 people. We don't really know why there are more MSEs in some places than others. Their existence is probably mainly dictated by need, though affluence and leisure may also act as driving forces for anti-crime and cultural groups.

MSEs are very diverse, and we have been reluctant to attempt a definition. But the project's advisors insisted that unless we did so, they would not believe that MSEs really existed as a distinct part of the

1

spectrum from friends to formal charities. So here is a working definition. An MSE is a coherent and effective community group that does not have any of the following:

- *staff*: people working full time, with job titles and salaries
- *office*: regular premises, equipment, stationery and business cards
- *funding*: dependable ongoing income of any significance
- *formalities*: legal definitions, registered charity numbers or 'agms'

To make up for this, what the low flying heroes are team of people with a great idea, boundless enthusiasm, and the nous to make things happen.

There is a big debate about whether social enterprise is currently on the rise – or is waning.[2] Whichever is the case, there is no doubt that it has been around for a long time. But it is no surprise that outfits without any of the visible attributes of a 'proper' organisation – the micro social enterprises – should have been consistently overlooked in the debate.

Don't be so formal

If an MSE is very ambitious, does very well and has a very charismatic leader, it may receive some recognition for its work. Management guru Charles Handy's recent book *The New Alchemists* celebrates entrepreneurs of all shapes and sizes. Tony Gibson of the Neighbourhood Initiatives Foundation, who has himself done a huge amount to support local neighbourhood initiatives, calls them 'prime movers'. Michael Young, the dazzling entrepreneur behind the Open University, Consumers' Association and numerous other social enterprises, has even set up a special School for Social Entrepreneurs.

Even the popular media will take notice of social entrepreneurs if they are as colourful or successful as business entrepreneurs like Richard Branson, Anita Roddick or James Dyson. A handful of especially successful social enterprises, such as Liam Black and the Furniture Resource Centre in Merseyside, have been featured on BBC Radio 4, and many people must by now have heard of Andrew Mawson's well-

---

What is social enterprise?

Social enterprise is the new buzz-word, but what exactly is it?

Enterprise has two meanings, which can cause confusion. The first suggests a relentless drive for profit and business success: the entrepreneur as tycoon. The second, older sense suggests a significant level of planned innovation in getting a new product or service off the ground.[3] While most MSEs make no profit by default as much as by choice, a significant minority may be planning to trade in future.

In a recent review of the international literature on social enterprise, Charles Edwards of the Open University Business School observes that traditional entrepreneurs 'do something new for the purpose of creating wealth and adding value'... In contrast, social entrepreneurs 'do something new with the aim of solving a social problem and adding social value'... In either case, the enterprises are innovative and dynamic agents of change. They see gaps in the market or perceive unmet needs in society, and invent or source creative products and services to address them.

Given the predominance of start-ups, more often than not the individuals concerned have never before run a business or managed an organisation. Inspiration and perspiration make up for the lack of previous experience or management training. The key strength of social enterprises large or small lies in an uncanny ability to think laterally and network intelligently. And on the rare occasions when they can't, they always seem to 'know a man or woman who can ...'

Source: Charles Edwards, Open University

---

publicised work at the Bromley-by-Bow Centre. Ironically, though, the individuals and organisations that come to public attention have by then, almost by definition, already ceased to be low flying heroes and have become high fliers.

New Economics Foundation – which itself started life in 1986 as a micro social enterprise in a Battersea flat – wrote a report called *Practical People,*

Noble Causes about such community-based social entrepreneurs in 1998. Many of the individuals featured in that report have already become professional community development workers or policy advisers. Some people are beginning to worry about the elitist connotations of the label.

But recently, things have been hotting up for the many common-or-garden MSEs too. Despite the difficulties of finding MSEs on the ground, the Millennium Commission and other grant-makers have funded a large number of award schemes. These schemes hand out 'small grants' (say £500–5,000) which 'enable individual people to put their bright ideas into action, fulfilling a personal goal, and, in doing so, benefiting their communities'.[4] The Scarman Trust neatly captures the spirit of the MSEs by calling the recipients Can-Doers. Recently it has teamed up with six other organisations to form unLTD, a scheme to support up to 1,500 social entrepreneurs a year all around the country, using an endowment from the Millennium Commission of £100 million.

Such support is flavour of the month, with over 50 schemes now providing support running to millions of pounds a year. But as NEF director Ed Mayo has said,[5] there is a danger that this is like cutting the tape on an array of shiny new bicycles, launched without having built the cycleways and paths they will need if they are to go far.

The first big cheque

A cheque for £2,000 could often be the largest sum the low flying heroes have ever received, by far. This is a moment which can throw up tensions between individual and group effort and reward. Is the cheque – and the media attention – for an individual social entrepreneur, a dynamic partnership or a broader community group? What should it be spent on?

Getting the cheque opens a new phase. It is just the start of a new journey full of opportunity and risk, confusion and excitement. Grant funding and press coverage are, unfortunately, far from being the answer to all their problems. For some MSEs, this is a crucial rite of passage into fully-fledged charities with growing impacts. For others it is the beginning of the end. Nor can support from local government, businesses or even the voluntary sector be taken for granted. These organisations can be unwittingly obstructive, or deliberately hostile.

Apart from the cash, other forms of support are being set up, or at least talked about. The Government's new national strategy for neighbourhood renewal contains dozens of concrete ideas, and the dynamic-sounding Neighbourhood Renewal Unit and Active Community Unit are finding their feet. Regional development agencies are busily undertaking surveys of the social economy; local government is rethinking its relationship with community activists.

This all sounds great; and not before time. We have seen decades of frequent failure and rare success by outside agencies intervening in the fight for regeneration, social inclusion and environmental sustainability. Finally, we seem to be recognising the need to support micro-social enterprises as being a highly effective agents of change, not just in our 3,000 most deprived neighbourhoods, but across the board. But do we *really* know how to do it?

An unknown quantity

The main difficulty of studying, let alone trying to support, low flying heroes is their sheer numbers, microscopic size and wide diversity.

Fully 87 per cent of the population are members of some group or other, or volunteer at least occasionally, according to the latest British Attitudes Survey.[6] Over 22 million people occasionally get out and volunteer in Britain's 20,000 communities; one in five adults do it regularly. At least four million people use community buildings every week in England and Wales. Over half a million people work for formal voluntary organisations. So there is such a thing as society, after all. Some even argue that activism is on the up: journalist Jonathan Freedland writes of a new 'us' generation taking over from the selfish 'me' generation.[7] Somewhere in this sliding scale of the active community are the low flying heroes.

We have already attempted to define them, but often a concrete example works better. Here is one story that gives a flavour of what we mean.

Allens Croft Community Story Telling Garden

Story telling is becoming a lost art. Years ago, before our modern information revolution, history and tradition were passed on through stories. Birmingham's Allens Croft estate is a little bit of history. The returning soldiers from World War I were famously promised "homes fit for heroes". A few years later came the first estates to be built by local authorities. The Pineapple Estate was Birmingham's pioneer. The estate was laid out in 1922 with wide streets, green spaces and solidly built family houses. Their white rendering gave the estate its nickname of the "White City" and to families moving there from the city slums it was a sort of paradise.

1997 was the estate's 75th birthday. In keeping with the vision of the times, the planners had included a youth club, the Pines. Old club members, most now pensioners, were contacted and many agreed to tell the modern day youngsters stories about the estate that the children could record and retell. Some children were as mischievous then as now. The old estate school's outside toilets were surrounded by an eight foot high wall. Those boys who could manage to pee over it were greatly respected.

Eileen Jordan and Barbara Eames both had a keen interest in the history of the estate, now renamed Allens Croft. The idea for the Community Story Telling Garden came to them as they looked at a piece of overgrown land next to the playground of the school. Somehow the trees and shrubs seem to suggest forgotten patterns and the two women, both pensioners, decided to try and set up a project to clear the brambles and weeds and establish a garden for the children.

As volunteers from the estate began the job of tidying and clearing, a hidden path came to light. Excited by this, Eileen and Barbara contacted more residents who had moved away and discovered that many could remember when the neglected area was in fact a garden between the wars. The lost art of story telling was to take place in the estate's lost garden.

Now the work is almost finished. The trees and shrubs are tidy and all the old pathways have been restored. A pergola and a decorative octagonal flower bed form the centre piece of the garden. Enough money has been raised to bring back the community story teller whose skills captured the imagination of even the toughest youngsters on the estate during the summer activity programme.

This bringing together of young and not so young is a key to the project's success. Elders are a huge resource to any neighbourhood, elders who can relate to youngsters and find common interests are even more so. Barbara and her husband are completing a book on the social history of the whole area. Eileen's husband, Alf, having just retired from working in the nearby Rover factory, has become the garden's site agent and is determined to see the job through. The school has an extra resource that will offer new experiences to the children who will become the next generation of story tellers.

Source: interview with Chris Wadhams, 1999

Such small-scale local activities can be hard to spot. How should they be supported? Should they be supported at all? Can merit be gauged by achievement, income, number of people involved, purposes, legal or constitutional structure, or what? Should the Active Community Unit and Neighbourhood Renewal Unit use a checklist to map this diverse range of voluntary, charitable and social business trading activity? How large a sector are we talking about? What obstacles does it face, and what are its needs? Or is it best left alone?

These are some of the questions and issues that the Joseph Rowntree Foundation asked us to explore. We did this first by looking at the fairly scant literature on the subject. We then used Scarman Trust Can Do awards information and other local knowledge to track down and listen carefully to dozens of micro-social enterprises in two very different places: Birmingham and Hastings. We also encouraged larger organisations to think back to the 'good old, bad old days' when they were smaller.

A pat on the back for government

Our fieldwork coincided with the policy action team ('PAT 9') assembled by the Government's Social Exclusion Unit to study community self-help. They concluded that 'Although there is considerable agreement about the main features of effective approaches – notably the need to engage the energy, commitment and leadership potential within the communities affected, and to ensure ownership of initiatives – policy makers have struggled to turn this into a usable template.' The national strategy for neighbourhood renewal and the new unit at DETR will be taking on the task of developing that template. This report concludes with ideas for what it should contain.

Before we examine what we discovered about those needs in detail, we look to India to gain some perspective on what is going on in the UK. This opens up an examination of the rich historical underpinnings that the emerging debate on the social economy has tended to overlook.

Next follows a review of the recent literature – such as it is – on self help and mutual aid and the implications for rethinking both the welfare state and the role of the traditional voluntary sector.

We then turn to the parallels and possible policy lessons from the micro-enterprise sector. The identity crisis suffered by new ventures in the market may be shared by those in civil society and those in the uncharted territory between the two. Finally, we review some contradictory recent estimates of the possible scale of micro social enterprise and attempt our own estimate based on a consolidation of different data.

A passage from India

It often seems to take a foreign eye to gain insights on a complex situation, as journalist Jonathan Freedland showed so successfully with his recent bestseller *Bring Home the Revolution*. Freedland learned from Alexis de Toqueville. This 19th century Frenchman visited and made a largely positive assessment of 'civic engagement' in the United States. Freedland's book argues that the US has retained very high levels of community activism, which have kept its democratic institutions vibrant and effective. De Toqueville was not so impressed with British institutions, and Freedland also finds them stagnant – though he has most recently detected glimmers of a renaissance in community activism; the possible rise of a new 'us' generation.[8] We have been similarly inspired by Sheela Patel's more recent – but less enthusiastic – assessment of the state of community regeneration in the UK.

In 1996, Sheela Patel of the Indian community group SPARC was asked by the Centre for Innovation and Voluntary Action and Oxfam to visit community regeneration initiatives in Glasgow, Edinburgh, Birmingham, Sandwell, Coventry, and London. Many of these had 'benefited' from major urban regeneration projects like City Challenge, Task Forces and their Scottish counterparts.

Her report made challenging reading. While she identified a good number of individual projects that looked to be working in their own limited terms of reference, Patel's analysis was that the British approach to regeneration was fundamentally flawed.

Patel described the predicament faced by Indian organisations in the early 1980s. As a consequence of rapid urbanisation, groups were simply overwhelmed with the scale of poverty and the needs of growing populations of slum dwellers and pavement dwellers. SPARC and other dynamic Indian groups grew out of the analysis of the inadequacy of service delivery models of relief or charitable provision. They simply refused to operate any longer in a 'top down' way.

Patel found the same predicament here in the UK. Her report made the following trenchant diagnosis:

- Urban regeneration is central government led and controlled; and regulatory disempowerment is common (e.g. informal child care services are declared illegal because of lack of qualified staff), while benefits traps like the infamous 48 hour rule block participation;

- Large amounts of money are made available for newly formed organisations; there is an emphasis on technology and a commodity fetishism of phones, faxes, computers and the latest gadgetry (which appears to be principally used to audit their work rather than to serve the goal of community empowerment);

- Voluntary organisations compete with each other counter-productively, hoarding knowledge and scarce information; local culture and 'know how' have been displaced by a 'culture of bids';

- Accountability of community regeneration organisations is not to community groups or local members but to government; bureaucracy and report writing is at a premium and at least 25 percent of work is consumed in audit enquiries required by government;

- The regeneration project staff are young; under-40s have little experience of mass mobilisation or protest organising;

- The insecurity of project funding and the continuous accountability to the state makes for a lack of confidence among project staff worried about losing their precarious employment;

- There is an emphasis on meetings rather than on action; capacity building courses focus on how to run meetings and apply for money; and

- The prevailing ethos is that value comes from either the market or the state rather than from people and their own culture.

Patel went on to offer some constructive ideas on a new agenda, based on SPARC's success in developing 'horizontal learning networks'. The principles of this strategy are that:

● Development does not trickle down;

● Local people actually know what the solutions are;

● There should be no hidden agendas or pre-planned strategies;

● Service provision and development are both needed but they do not co-exist easily;

● Real things need to be allowed to progress slowly and at a human pace of trial and error.

In putting these principles into practice in India over the past 15 years, SPARC has insisted on the need for a decentralised approach and on the need to share knowledge and information among all development and community organisations by putting it in the public domain. They also learned that there are no formulas or manuals to teach development – it is a process of imagination, risk taking, experimentation and non-specialisation. [9]

Historical underpinnings

Interest in strengthening and enabling just such an active civil society was rekindled in the lead up to the election of New Labour in 1997. The scale of the electoral victory was an endorsement of the popular feeling generated by Blair, Prescott and Brown for a new social contract beyond the opening gambit of the 'New Deal'. There was, resoundingly, such a thing as society. Yet at the end of the century, the Third Way of New Labour still seemed elusive.

Labour think tanks had begun to notice the untapped potential of the social economy, and community action emerged as a key part of the national strategy for neighbourhood renewal. But while the late 1990s literature contained many good ideas, the social economy was seldom defined. Nor were self-help and mutual aid clearly distinguished from each other. As most were happy to acknowledge, local community action was hardly discovered by late 1990s spin doctors on government task forces.

So before describing and trying to interpret the current community enterprise activities in Birmingham and Hastings, profiled in the next section, it's worth looking a little further back into the history of community groups. Readers with little appetite for history, who want to get straight on to the case studies, should proceed immediately to page 23.

Mutuality, market and state

For over two centuries, co-operative development, the historic form of social enterprise, has been waxing and waning in Britain. Co-operation has been an alternating current responding to social crisis by kicking in with alternative, socially inclusive forms of work and enterprise. It was Edmund Burke, reflecting on the French Revolution, who noted that 'To be attached to the subdivision, to love the little platoon we belong to in society, is the first principle, the germ, as it were, of public affections. It is the first link in the series by which we proceed toward a love to our country and to mankind.'[10] Co-operation within the little platoons may even predate the industrial market economy. EP Thompson, Ivan Illich and Aldous Huxley are among those who argued that it was a survival of pre-capitalist societies.

Mutualisation more broadly pre-dates the 19th century co-operative societies by over 2000 years. In ancient Rome, mutual savings clubs, *collegia*, developed sickness and burial insurance for the working class. In the early Middle Ages, guilds often produced goods that were needed for the local economy, not at a market price, but at a 'just' price – fixed to provide a fair return for a skilled craftsman.[11]

Reciprocity or mutual aid was the non-commercial exchange of goods and labour through gifting and barter; individual self-interest was anathema in pre-capitalist society. Faith was placed in God, each other and the productivity of the land rather than in money, the market and the state. Social reciprocity is still observable today among family and friends and underlies the gifting rituals of birthdays, weddings, leaving events, and religious festivals on the one hand, and the gifting of alms and time through religious and lay volunteering and self-help groups on the other.

The Pioneers: co-operative development in perspective

You could sometimes be forgiven for thinking that community self-help was a late 20th century invention, but it was when trade with the North American colonies was impeded in the 1760s, due to war with the French, that the first European co-operative was established to provide flour in Woolwich, London.

As a result of the economic hardships caused by both the second trade war with America from 1812 to 1814 and the public debt of the Napoleonic Wars, Robert Owen's call for 'Villages of Cooperation' in 1817 triggered a worldwide movement. Trade Unions, initially organised covertly as Friendly Societies in the late 18th century, emerged more widely during the Depression of the early 1830s, and led by Robert Owen formed the Grand National Consolidated Trade Union.

It was Benjamin Franklin who said 'Time is money'; this period also saw the first large scale experiment with interest-free co-operative money based on hours – the pioneer of today's alternative currency systems. From 1832 to 1834, Labour Notes were traded by the National Equitable Labour Exchanges established to relieve unemployment in Grays Inn, London and Bull Street, Birmingham by Owenite socialists.

In the 'hungry 1840s', the Rochdale Pioneers developed their eight principles for co-operation, paving the way for the mighty consumer cooperative movement that advanced hand in glove with Trade Unionism until the First World War. John Stuart Mill and the Christian Socialists put mutuality onto a sound, legally constituted basis with the support they gave to the co-operative movement, to establish the Industrial and Provident Societies Acts of 1852 and 1862. These recognised three forms of mutuality: worker co-operatives ('Industrial Societies'), consumer co-operatives ('Provident Societies') and a third category, social co-operatives ('Societies for Community Benefit').

Against the growth of large-scale manufacturing, worker co-operative advocates within and without the Trade Union movement continued to pursue their vision of worker self-management across Europe, but this was effectively suppressed or eclipsed by the rise of Communism, Fascism and Social Democracy in the 1920s–30s. Indeed, with the decline of small businesses in Britain in the 50-year period 1915–65, co-operation declined as well.

The deep recession of the early 1980s and the rapid growth of self-employment and small businesses in the mid 1980s saw the first new growth period of worker co-operatives, housing co-operatives, and community co-operatives since the early 1920s. Most recently, the recession of the early 1990s witnessed in the UK a huge growth of credit unions to over 800 and local currency systems (LETS, Time Banks etc) to over 500, a trend which looks set to survive – and even thrive – in the early 21st century.

Source: Pat Conaty

Formal charity grew out of these ancient practices, as did the welfare state in this century. This vibrant legacy of self-help and mutual aid culture seems to have been largely forgotten in the recent policy debate, and with it some useful lessons.

Self-help and mutual aid: recent research

In one of the most comprehensive reviews of current patterns of self-help and mutual aid activities, Burns and Taylor (Joseph Rowntree Foundation, 1998) define self-help as activity by individuals for themselves or their family and mutual aid as activity that involves reciprocity between people. Examples include neighbourhood care, community literacy schemes, allotment growing, informal savings clubs, shared childcare, Local Exchange Trading Schemes (LETS), soup kitchens, community protection schemes and a wide range of self-help groups.

In Burns and Taylor's view, such organisations:

- are based on informal group structures or networks;
- are based on direct rather than representative forms of decision making;
- have no formal relationship to the state; and
- have no staff and do not assign work according to formal rules.

Burns and Taylor also highlight three key ways in which mutual aid and self-help are used by disadvantaged communities. Firstly, they are used directly to solve problems. Secondly, they act as a springboard or nurture a start up phase for initiatives that can progress into the mainstream either as a voluntary organisation or, in some cases, as a business. Thirdly, they often operate as an alternative to the mainstream.

Self-help and mutual aid activities also help people to acquire skills that can frequently lead to employment or the confidence to start a business. Some mutual aid efforts can deliver all three purposes. For example, Burns and Taylor show how squatting is a direct solution to a housing problem. It provides stability and an address which can then act as a springboard to a job. It provides a viable alternative to conventional forms of housing tenure that might not be available.

Both public and voluntary sectors have ambivalent views towards self-help and mutual aid groups, with the state trying to regulate or even suppress them and the formal voluntary sector feeling threatened by them or tending to ignore them. As with trading in the informal economy, mutual aid occasionally embraces both romantic and illegal practices. Burns and Taylor refer to controversial activities such as vigilantism. In these days when grant makers increasingly seek evidence of grass roots participation in service development, attempts to co-opt or take over mutual aid or self-help groups can easily kill them off.

In conclusion, Burns and Taylor caution against most policy interventions – which they consider are more likely to do more harm than good. The best assistance possible is to help create a benign environment for development and to offer, very carefully, indirect help through either self-help or community development agency support that is sensitive to the group needs.

But the self-sufficient vibrancy of the self-help sector should not be taken for granted. In another large study looking at the self-help activity among 400 households in four low-income neighbourhoods – two in Sheffield and two in Southampton – Williams and Windebank (1999) challenge the cosy assumption that the unemployed are likely to use their 'spare time' to start micro social enterprises. Indeed their research finds exactly the opposite.

Barriers to self help activity amongst those unemployed include:

● lack of money and access to equipment;

● lack of people they could call on for help (a social network);

● lack of skills, confidence or physical abilities to engage in self-help;

● a fear of being reported to the Benefits Agency and losing their entitlement to Social Security;

● lack of confidence in the local community and a sense of isolation.

Wilson (1995) dramatically highlights the two worlds of community self-help groups and professionals.

Worlds apart: self-help groups and professionals

	Self help groups	Professionals
Structure	Informal	Formal
Decision making	Participative	Hierarchical
Main concern	Mutual support and information	Provision of services
Source of knowledge	Through experience	Through training
Degree of permanence	Uncertain	Long term
Reward for time	Better coping; Satisfaction from being helpful	Pay and status; Satisfaction from being helpful
Resources	Volunteer help Members' homes	Paid staff Offices
Degree of integration to structures	Low	High
Language	Everyday	Jargon/shorthand

Mai Wann (1995) drew attention to the radical cultural character and prospects of self-help:

'Self-help has much in common with voluntarism and charity: people doing things for others without prospect of commercial gain and out of a desire to make the world a better place to live in. However, there are essential differences. Self-help is not primarily about altruism or philanthropy; it is not about helping others less fortunate than oneself. It is about self-determination and co-operation and those who are involved in the same boat. It can be seen as part of the voluntary sector, but while most traditional voluntary organisations are paternalist, self-help groups are, in essence, liberationist. They are about people making their own choices and taking control over their lives.'

Barry Knight suggests that the voluntary sector as a whole has been through a number of phases since 1945 (CAF, 1998). He suggests that the first cycle, from 1945 to 1965, was a period of defensive decline. The next phase, from 1966 to 1978 was a period of rebirth and advocacy. The most recent phase from 1979 to 1998 has been one of service delivery. In his analysis, signs of a rejuvenated, more effective phase are also now becoming visible.

There are signs that a revival of co-operative development did indeed begin in the 1970s and picked up in the recession of the early 1980s, gaining voice in the tough Thatcher years. The recent record has been patchy, though. Building societies have actually been demutualising at a rate of knots (although Nationwide said 'no', and Standard Life, valued at £19 billion is a mutual too). Worker co-operatives, with just 15,000 employees, have not revived very impressively since the recession of the early 1990s, either. And the Co-op is losing market share too.

But other forms of co-operation, self-help and mutual aid have advanced. Recent research by Charlie Leadbeater, Ian Christie and Ed Mayo has highlighted a new mutualism with more emphasis on social co-operatives ('societies for community benefit') by contrast to the more traditional friendly societies, building societies, mutual insurers, consumer and agricultural co-operatives.

The new mutualism includes over 3,000 plus self-help and mutual aid groups in health, almost 19,000 pre-school groups and mutual kids' clubs, 120,000 neighbourhood watch groups, 400 mediation schemes and crime prevention partnerships, 584 credit unions, 193 development trusts and community foundations, 120,000 housing co-operative units, 20,000 members of LETS schemes, and 210 tenant management co-ops and self build schemes (Demos, 1999). These are quite impressive numbers for a sector said to be in decline.

According to Mai Wann (IPPR, 1995), the biggest growth has occurred in the last ten years. She characterises (some would say caricatures) the radicalism of the movement that is 'building social capital' in this way:

> *'This renaissance of self help in the late 20th century coincides with a time of crisis and reappraisal for post-war welfarism, and*

with a time of diminishing public confidence in traditional representative democracy. It can be seen as a response to the failure of centralism and paternalism, two powerful tendencies which have helped to shape Western welfare democracies. Yet it also challenges the ideals of neo-liberalism. It involves individuals combining in small groups to provide for each other what the market cannot provide. Self help... is about sharing knowledge, skills, and power – the antithesis of a marketplace where the fittest survive and the weakest go to the wall.'

So, writers like Wann, Taylor, Burns, Windebank, Williams and others have all observed an upsurge of self help and mutual aid activity in the 1990s. It is clear, both from the history and recent literature, that renewing an active civil society will not be quick, easy or cheap. Government and trust funding for the sector has been substantial over the past decade, but there is little evidence that existing forms of community development have had much effect in reducing social exclusion (Robson, 1995; Knight and Stokes, 1998).

So can the MSEs break this cycle of local regeneration failure? Or will the 'low flying heroes' of neighbourhood renewal, quietly (sometimes surreptitiously) trying to get on with their work, get caught out on the radar screen of unrealistic expectations, jealous partners and Whitehall red tape?

Micro-enterprise: an identity crisis?

So much for community self-help; what about economic help-yourself? In the developing world, micro-enterprise is the norm rather than the exception in terms of employment and visible activity for profit. Here, formal and informal economic activity blend into one another and registered or legal enterprises are totally over-shadowed in, say, Guatemala City or Calcutta by countless street sellers and cottage industries of all descriptions. Worldwide, there are estimated to be over 3 billion micro-enterprises, which employ over half the world's workforce.

In Britain, too, micro-enterprise activity is not only proliferating but becoming, in low income neighbourhoods, one of the few employment opportunities available. Indeed, Department of Trade and Industry (DTI) figures show that over one-third of non-government employment in the UK is now with micro-enterprises and that this sector is the fastest growing area of new employment. This is true not only in Britain, but in most OECD countries as well.

Napoleon was right; we are a nation of shopkeepers. Despite the fact that ten local shops are closing very day, micro-enterprise is back on the agenda. According to statistics from the DTI, there are over 3.7 million businesses in the UK. Of these, 2.4 million (67 per cent) are one-person businesses with no other employees. A further 1.1 million are micro-enterprises with nine employees or less. Only 32,000 firms in the UK (less than one per cent) employ more than 50 people. Of these, only 1,200 or so are registered on the Stock Exchange. Yet the business pages of the media are preoccupied with just a few hundred firms and their merger-mania.[12]

Hardly surprising that micro-enterprise has long had an identity crisis – especially during the early formative years. This is exacerbated by their embryonic, fragile, informal and legally unconstituted characteristics, as well as to their intermediate and frequently part-time nature. They are somewhere between a hobby and self-employment. Economic development strategies still refer to the 'problem' of sole traders; Arthur Daley's sheepskin coat is the emblem of the sector's disreputable, naughty-but-nice nature.

It is not just lack of recognition behind the identity crisis. It is also driven by the short life-expectancy of most micro-enterprises, which is, dauntingly, under two years. Forget the press stories of the dazzling success of James Dyson and Slelios, EasyJet chairman. According to the DTI, in 1997 there were 508,000 new businesses started; in the same year 489,000 folded.[13]

There is, however, a potential role for government and big business to help the micro-enterprise sector overcome its identity crisis and live up to its potential. Help is needed in four key areas, according to a recent report on business sector micro-enterprise (Conaty & Fisher, NEF, 1999):

- Flexible funding

- Overcoming obstacles

- Promoting partnerships

- Education for entrepreneurship

On a positive note, the rising contribution of the small business sector has been increasingly recognised, and significant sums are now expended by the DTI and other government departments to assist both new and established small businesses to grow and thrive. The forthcoming Small Business Service certainly helps, particularly if more attention can be paid to the important differences between small and micro businesses, so that the service can deliver for both.

By contrast, little attention from a policy point of view has been focused on the ill-defined micro-social enterprise sector. The DTI knows that corporate giants such as Hewlett Packard and Microsoft started life from garage premises or the kitchen table top. But there appears to be little comparable awareness yet by the Department of Environment, Transport and the Regions (DETR) and Home Office of how the same humble origins in the voluntary sector can, with the right support, lead to medium or large organisations (as well as large numbers of small ones).

But before working out what sorts of support would be applicable to the needs of micro-social enterprises, we need to know a little more about them. First things first, how many are there?

How many micro-social enterprises are there?

Experts all agree on one thing: nobody really knows how many micro-social enterprises (MSEs) there are in the UK. Even in the more formal, large scale end of the voluntary sector, numbers are vague. The Deakin Report famously reported in 1996 that 'recent estimates of the numbers of active organisations have ranged from 170,000 to 1.3 million'.

These vague ballpark figures are confirmed by a number of recent, local mapping studies.

The numbers game: counting low flying heroes

There are 187,000 formal charities with an income on the Charity Commission register for England and Wales. Using pro rata figures for Scotland and Northern Ireland would give a total of some 218,000 registered charities in the UK as a whole.[14] Two thirds of these organisations have an annual income of less than £10,000, and the Deakin Report on the future of the voluntary sector warned that this group of lower income organisations might be facing the need to 're-voluntarise'. What about the already voluntarised, informal, unregistered, unrecognised community groups, though?

Jeremy Kendall, an expert at the London School of Economics, thinks the proportion of small to large organisations in the voluntary sector is even higher than in the business sector. Using a broad definition, which includes educational establishments, places of worship, housing associations, recreation and business associations, he and Knapp have estimated some 140–180,000 small groups. This does not include very informal local groups, either.[15]

Research in Scotland suggests 18,000 voluntary groups without formal charitable status, such as churches, trusts and playgroups. This means there is more than one informal group for every two formal ones.[16] If this ratio applied to the other three countries as there are in Scotland, relative to the formal sector, there would be around 150,000 informal voluntary groups in the UK.

Gabriel Chanan of the Community Development Foundation reckons that across Europe there are on average at least three community groups or voluntary organisations per 1000 people. 'Nearly all local voluntary organisations are small', note CDF, 'but the research suggests that there are large numbers of very small local organisations, whether formally constituted or not, mostly indigenous to the locality, and smaller numbers of relatively large organisations, a higher proportion of which would be formally constituted and/or may be branches of national charities or projects initiated by public authorities... So, for example, a [town with] 25,000 population is likely to have approximately 75 groups and organisations. Most of these are likely to be community groups, and many will be small and isolated' (Chanan, 1994; Chanan & West, 1999).

Using CDF's conservative three per 1000 people rule of thumb would give a total for the UK of 180,000 such groups. The Charities Aid Foundation push it a bit higher still, believing there could be at least 200,000 informal organisations. But they are not sure. 'The omission of community groups from most major surveys is an ever more significant gap', admits Cathy Pharaoh in *Dimensions of the Voluntary Sector*, 1998.

These local studies show anywhere from three to 20–25 groups per thousand local people. Last year's PAT 9 report suggested between three and six as a consensus, but maybe as little as two in socially excluded areas, while Konrad Elsdon and others have disputed this, believing there could be 13–15 groups per thousand people even on deprived estates.[17]

Taking a conservative midway range of 10–15 MSEs per thousand people gives an estimated 600,000–900,000 micro social enterprises for the country as a whole – which is three or more times as many as the formal charities. Assuming that on average three to six people are actively involved in each enterprise, this makes between 1.8 million and 5.4 million people actively involved in MSEs.[18] These are impressive numbers for a largely invisible part of society, flying below the public policy radar screen.

Some recent local studies of voluntary & community groups

Place/Study	No. of groups	Groups / 1000 people
Gloucestershire	Experts estimate anywhere from 1,500–15,000 in population of 553,000)	3–30
Southwark	900 groups for population of 232,000	4
Devon & Cornwall	5,387 (+ maybe 500–1,000 MSEs) in population of 1.54 m	3.5–4.2
Newham	1,000 in a population of 215,000	5
LOVAS (16 places)	Various	13
Retford (+ 31 other places)	Various	20–25

Sources: LRPD / PRI for PROSPER, 1998; Greg Smith, 1998; SAVO, 1999; Gloucestershire Network, 1999; Home Office website, 2000; Elsdon *et al.*, 1995

But the uncertainty is impressive, too. It makes it impossible to devise an adequate support package. Nor do we really know much about what sorts of support should be in that package. If money is the main need, how much is needed and for how many groups? And if it's not, then what else can be done?

The PAT report suggested a target of increasing numbers of groups by 50%, and increasing the number of people involved in groups threefold, from 5% of local people to 15%. Not knowing how many groups there are is a crucial area of policy uncertainty, given the stated government intention to support MSEs in deprived areas, and plans to help set up new ones. It's just not possible to judge whether the levels of support being talked about will be adequate, but if unLTD is one of the more ambitious schemes, serving 1,500 entrepreneurs a year, it seems highly unlikely given potential demand of 600,000 groups or more. Given this uncertainty, it's disappointing but not surprising that the neighbourhood renewal strategy has not adopted these proposed targets.

The next section of the report describes how we went about meeting some individual low flying heroes, and what we learnt – from them – about their needs.

MEETING THE LOW FLYING HEROES

Our research approach

The name may be new, but everyone probably knows a couple of micro social enterprises. There are several in most communities. So it should be pretty easy to go out and meet a good number of them.

It certainly sounds straightforward enough. Gabriel Chanan & Alison West (1999) say that 'In a locality of up to 100,000 people, it should be possible to establish and survey all the reasonably stable, visible and active organisations that can be found, ie all the organisations that have an established name and contact address, a minimum of ten members or users, and which carried out some form of activity at least six times in the past year'. Konrad Elsdon, who knows more about this than most, gives many useful tips about how to establish a full list of organisations, including tramping around looking at notice boards and asking in pubs (Elsdon, 1998). Others have recommended bingo halls and the foyers to shopping centres as stamping grounds for community activists.

There have been several useful studies of community action on the ground, such as Barry Knight's 1993 Centris report on voluntary action, the Home Office's LOVAS surveys (1994–1999) and Elsdon's guide to *Studying Local Voluntary Organisations* (1998). With these and other one-area-specific studies, it is slowly becoming possible to answer key questions about MSEs.

Are there hotbeds of MSE activity in certain areas, or over time? Is high density mainly an urban or a rural phenomenon; and what gender, racial and class differences should be expected? What sorts of issues galvanise most activity? Is density correlated with income or deprivation; is it a middle class luxury or a lifeline for the socially excluded? Which types are most effective; how many people do they involve? These and many other questions need to be answered in full statistical fashion. The PAT 9 recommendation that local 'audits' of voluntary activity be undertaken, by faith groups and others that are already established in communities, was very timely; but apart from NEF's recent report *Charitable Trust*,[19] there is hardly any experience of social auditing in the informal voluntary sector.

This project had the modest goal of finding out some qualitative information, and we narrowed the field as much as possible, by concentrating on just two places in England. These were a West Midlands city, Birmingham, and a South Coast town, Hastings. These were not intended to be 'representative' of Britain in any sense,[20] although both are relevant to the regeneration agenda and have their fair share of neighbourhoods needing renewal.

Nor did we try to audit all the MSEs in our two areas. Birmingham is much too big: there could be five thousand or more. And Hastings, with a more manageable 80,000 inhabitants, and perhaps just 300–400 groups, is far too hilly to walk around and has a disproportionate number of pubs to check out.

In any case, we did not plan a statistical analysis of MSEs by sending them a questionnaire in the mail. Our assumption was that the smaller groups we were most interested in were least likely to respond to a questionnaire. What we wanted was to spend time listening carefully to the stories of a few dozen MSEs, and be able to add some qualitative information to the policy debate.

By coincidence, both the West Midlands and Sussex had been the focus of an award called Can Do. These are awards of £2,000 given out by the Scarman Trust on behalf of the Millennium Commission to Can Doers – 'hundreds of remarkable people who are determined to change their communities for the better'.[21] Can Doers fitted our definition of MSEs very well, and were also well placed to help identify other, not-so-lucky MSEs in their neighbourhood. In Birmingham we were also able to draw on the Quest Trust's Millennium Award scheme.

We also used local databases of voluntary organisations, although there is often a big gap between official lists and actually functioning groups on the ground. For example, none of the nine Can Doers in Hastings was until that point listed on the database of over 100 voluntary organisations kept at the Hastings Trust; sometimes groups only get onto a database once they have stopped being an MSE.

Once identified, we spent several hours talking to one or more people involved in each project. We used a so-called semi-structured interview (see annex), which helps the interviewer not to forget important questions, but allows a fairly natural conversation to develop. Telephone interviews did not work. Being busy people, MSEs are not always easy to track down. They may, with good reason, be wary of unknown researchers. Even so, people seemed often to enjoy the opportunity of telling their stories.

Over the summer of 1999, we undertook 20 detailed interviews with MSEs: twelve in Birmingham and eight in Hastings. We also spoke at length to a number of highly successful people (the 'high-fliers') who had been in similar positions in the past, asking them to think back to the 'good old, bad old days'.

The result was that we began to understand a little more about the experience of MSEs. We saw for ourselves the broad range of activities they are involved in. We realised that each was on a unique development path. We plainly saw that each thrives on its own interplay of individual and group energies and we heard that an insurmountable problem for one was a golden opportunity for another.

The amazing diversity of the low-flying heroes is the main finding of our work. Surely this is obvious? Well, yes, in a way it is. But the trouble with many of the existing studies is that they pay lip-service to this important fact, and then go on to propose a uniform prescription for all groups. Yes, they come in all shapes and sizes, but one size must fit all.

This report shows the need for a more flexible treatment. But first, there are some gross generalisations to make about this diversity.

What are they getting up to?

Our interviews showed that the MSEs are involved in a very wide range of activities, from organic gardens to community launderettes, from credit unions to rap music, from bonfires to video history. Can any pattern be discerned?

Looking at the objectives of the 96 Can Do award winners from the West Midlands and Sussex, a third are active in the very broad category of recreation, leisure and arts (32%). A quarter are providing social services, while a good number are working on economic (14%) and environmental (12%) issues. Many fewer Can Doers are working on housing and education. Not surprisingly, few are attempting general policy work. More surprisingly, 8% were working on community development. Until very recently, community development was actually ruled out as a charitable activity!

Indicative breakdown of MSE activity in West Midlands & Sussex

Area	*Scarman Can Doers: numbers tackling issue (%)*
Recreation/leisure/arts	32
Social services	25
Economic development	14
Environment/planning	12
Community development	8
Education	4
Housing	3
Policy/general	2
Total	**100**

Source: Scarman Trust information/NEF analysis1999

This breakdown is based on just under 100 MSEs in the West Midlands and Sussex. A more thorough breakdown is urgently needed.[22] Nor could we find a comparable breakdown of activity in the larger, more formal voluntary and charity sector.[23] It is essential, says Konrad Elsdon, that categories in new studies are not 'too broad to be meaningful'.

So we simply do not know whether MSEs follow the activity pattern of the formal sector. Are they proportionately dealing more – or less – with social services than recreation; with religious issues than environment? There is no easy way to compare. What this means is that departmental policy makers in health, education, housing, crime or environment do not know whether the support packages they are talking about setting up for MSEs are proportionate to the demand.

Ladder or spectrum? the many paths of the low flying hero

There is a general expectation in policy and grant-giving circles that micro-social enterprises can – and so should – follow the tried and tested development path: raise some funds, get a computer, print stationery, hire a part time worker, find premises, get charitable status. Then onwards and upwards to being a 'real' voluntary sector organisation. But is this the right approach?

Researchers have usefully distinguished six types of community and voluntary activity:

- Family and neighbours
- Informal community action (ie the low flying heroes)
- Formal community action
- Mutual/economic groups
- Groups based on a community of interest
- 'Formal' voluntary organisations

The Social Exclusion Unit correctly notes that 'this range of involvement, from the most informal to the structured and formally constituted, is central to an understanding of community self-help'. But it goes on: 'There is a ladder or spectrum of community and voluntary activity.' This is a telling phrase which indicates a subconscious tension in thinking about MSEs. A ladder is meant for climbing, rung by rung, till you get to the right height: the top. But the colours in a spectrum are all equally important. Red is not low; violet is not higher.

'Ladder thinking' is prevalent in the debate about where informal groups ought to be going. But this has only rarely been challenged by 'spectrum thinking'. Several of our MSEs showed no real ambition, sometimes an aversion, to climb the ladder. They are happy as they are. RH Tawney long ago criticised the 'Tadpole Philosophy', where the conditions and needs of the majority were regarded as secondary to the needs of the tiny minority that will go on to become frogs. We simply do not know how many MSEs aspire to become frogs.

In *Organising around Enthusiasms*, Bishop and Hoggett talk about self-sustaining groups that derive their energy from mutual enthusiasms, such as pigeon-fancying. There are many such groups that are doing quite nicely (or bumping along the bottom, if you see it as a ladder) without any outside support at all. We only notice these groups when they collapse, like the recent demise of a village cricket club whose male players had finally exhausted the enthusiasm of the female sandwich-makers.

The existence of this other way of seeing organisations – as all equally valid on a spectrum – challenges the single growth model that is predominant. Instead of rungs on a ladder, we developed five hypothetical scenarios to try to open up the debate about where MSEs are heading.[24]

There is nothing inherently right or wrong with any of these scenarios – like different sports, it depends on your preference and the conditions. Each can be done well, or done badly. The picture opposite illustrates them, and the table gives a positive and negative 'spin' on each.

In case these scenarios seem too abstract, below is a case study of what we are calling a pole vaulter. As part of its Community Economic Development strategy, Birmingham City Council has significantly funded development agency support since the mid-1980s through voluntary sector bodies for credit unions, worker co-operatives, and community businesses. The Ladywood estate in inner Birmingham,

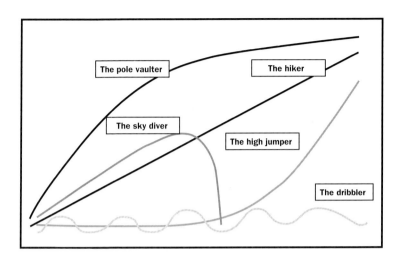

Scenario	Best case	Worst case
The pole vaulter	Up, up and away	Reached our limits
The hiker	Planned and steady growth	Long hard up and down slog
The high jumper	We finally made it	Third attempt at this height
The sky diver	Job done, time to move on	Crashed and burnt out
The dribbler	Keep it nice and tight	Bump along the bottom

through the work of the Ladywood Project and Co-Enterprise (the citywide community business support agency), has fostered the development of both the Ladywood Furniture Project and Babywood as successful community businesses. Babywood as a community nursery was initiated in June 1989 as a micro-social enterprise by two young unemployed women fed up by the lack of child care in Ladywood.

High Fliers: Babywood, just like a business

Summer 1989. Carol Coombes was 26 and unemployed with four young children. She had been living on the Ladywood Estate since 1982. The lack of nursery provision locally was a widespread complaint among young mums and Carol and her friend Sarah saw a flier and signed up for a course in community business development. After the first two course sessions, she and Sarah said to each other, 'Why not?' and the idea of Babywood was hatched. Between them, they mobilised 15 mums to form a steering group and recruited six from the group to work with them as volunteers to make it happen.

With the support of the Birmingham Voluntary Services Council, Carol was able to secure a European Social Fund training scheme allowance of £70 per week for Sarah and her to work on the business development full time. They both put in 'sweat equity' – often 90 hours a week in the first year – to get the community business off the ground.

The biggest headache was managing the expectations of their steering group. Some wanted jobs, others wanted free childcare, many wanted both and all wanted results quickly. Nonetheless, Carol and Sarah were a great team with complementary skills. Sarah was a good office manager and systems person. Carol had a penchant for marketing, recruiting volunteers and raising resources. 'The two of us were unassailable', they felt.

Most, in business terms, was achieved by trial and error. Business planning was not a bad idea and Carol was proud of her first cash flow forecast, only to find that, when it was put into practice, she had forgotten to include food expenditure; 'fancy running a ten hour nursery without any food.' For Carol, a 'Game Plan' was a better name than a 'Business Plan' … It took her, Sarah and the volunteers over two years to do all the preparations, secure a derelict building from the Council, raise grant aid to refurbish it and train and recruit the staff. They opened for business in October 1991 and today, Babywood is an 80 place nursery with 30 subsidised and 50 unsubsidised places and an annual turnover of £800,000 plus.

For Carol, it was the teamwork that made it work. Setting it up was hard, but not half as hard as running it. She sums it up: 'a community business is like any other business and needs to be run as a business. It is different from a conventional business because of social aims – but otherwise, just like any other business.'

Source: Interviewed by Pat Conaty, July 1999.

Three types of MSE?

Are all MSEs basically the same type of outfit? No. There seem to be (at least) three basic and different types.

The term 'social entrepreneur' has been coined to name individuals who use their brilliant ideas, passion and determination to promote social benefit rather than business profit. As a 1998 NEF report showed, social entrepreneurship is about practical people, noble causes. Social entrepreneurs are individualistic mavericks, the Dysons and Bransons of community development.

Some of the MSEs we interviewed were clearly social entrepreneurs in the making. Some of them have even 'made it' since we interviewed them. In October 1999, Keith Leech, the brains behind the Hastings Bonfire (see page 33) was awarded the Order of 1066, the highest honour the Borough of Hastings can award. For him, this has been quite a battle. He has worked with teams the whole way, but there is no doubting his central role.

But what about Carol and Sarah in Babywood? They do not fit the model of the brilliant but lonely social entrepreneur. If anything, they are more of a 'dynamic duo', unassailable in their togetherness. Several other of our interviews, like Sue and Tina with Kamara in Birmingham, or Jackie and Clare on the Ore Valley estate in Hastings, are partnerships like this. Just like Bill Gates and Paul Allen of Microsoft, or Hewlett-Packard.

But some of the MSEs we interviewed, such as the Hindu Women's Network, were neither sole entrepreneurs nor dynamic duos. These groups are more like football teams: with different skills and roles, and perhaps even a captain, but groups nonetheless.

This basic distinction between different organisational forms is obvious. But when MSEs are talked about, it sometimes gets forgotten. There is a growing debate between those that see social entrepreneurs and those that favour groups as the prime movers in communities. Support packages tend to be designed according to preference.

Yet it is very damaging to treat one half of a dynamic duo as a lone entrepreneur, and equally counter-productive to subject an entrepreneur to 'death by a thousand committees'. To complicate matters, an MSE may be in the process of changing from one type to another. Grant-makers and policy-makers must be crystal clear what sort of outfit they are dealing with. As yet, there are simply no tools to help, so it is hit-and-miss.

Three key ingredients for success

Our guided interviews covered a lot of ground, as the case above illustrates. When we came to look at them, though, we noticed that most of what was being discussed fell into three clear areas:

- **Inspiration:** a small group of people, galvanised by one very dynamic individual on a mission; or a team of equals fulfilling ambitions they had to put on hold while doing a first career or bringing up a child.

- **Resources:** how they gained access to money, but also the importance of workspace, advice and elbow grease; or how they coped without these.

- **Relationships:** with local residents, with the council (local government), with business, with the authorities (police, health and safety), with central government, with formal voluntary sector organisations, with each other.

As new economist Perry Walker puts it: 'just as the Internal Rate of Return is the key to a successful conventional business, the IRR formula of Inspiration, Resources and Relationships is crucial to community groups'. In the following three sections, we discuss each in turn, illustrated with case studies of MSEs in action for each. Where relevant, we also give some examples of 'high fliers': how bigger, more formal voluntary organisations have managed to succeed, with possible lessons for their smaller counterparts.

INSPIRATION

Low flying heroes are about 99 per cent inspiration, but they need 99 per cent perspiration too. It's not just having the idea; it's about keeping going, often for years, as Keith Leech shows.

Two big ideas: Keith Leech, the Jack in the Green & the Bonfire Society

When biology teacher Keith Leech won the Hastings Personality of the Year prize in 1997, it was the culmination of 15 years of inspiration and perspiration. The idea for a colourful Jack in the Green event on the May Day Bank holiday (JITG) was, Keith says, 'hatched in a pub' as a result of his passion for folk history, a network of like-minded friends and having a bit of time on his hands after moving from London.

Jack in the Green was run single-handedly for quite a long time, and only slowly built up popularity over a period of 10 years. Now run by a small committee, this 'excuse to get dressed up, make a noise and drink beer' is firmly established in the town's calendar and has become a magnet for folk enthusiasts from all over the country. Eventually, Keith dreams that people will start up events in other towns and cities, rather than keep returning to Hastings.

Not one to limit his energies, Keith founded and is still deeply involved in the Hastings Bonfire Society, which has 'literally exploded' in the last five years. More of a team effort from the start, there are half a dozen core people, 20 committed workers, and 200 helpers on the night, to cope with a crowd of 20,000 (a fifth of the town's population).

Keith loves getting positive feedback from people who attend the events, but has had to develop a thick skin to cope with 'artistic snobbery'. Purists question the cultural and social worthiness of the two carnivals and prefer to fund less populist events. Bonfires tend towards 'controlled anarchy', even when they do not have undertones of religious intolerance, a charge that has been levelled at the one in Lewes. So despite the close scrutiny of the council's Health and Safety people, the authorities remain at best lukewarm, while some religious groups are openly opposed to its apparent paganism. But if social capital is counted by sheer weight of numbers of people having a good time, the social contribution of Jack in the Green and the Bonfire has no rivals in Hastings. It also helps that the mayor is a big fan.

The fixed costs of JITG are now modestly funded by the council's tourism budget, but not Keith's time. Sponsorship might help: a similar event in Rochester nets the organiser about £10,000. The bonfire relies on year-long fundraising events and a grant of £1,000 from the council. 'There are times', Keith admits, 'when I feel I ought to be making these things much more commercial'. In common with many micro social enterprises, though, he is wary of sponsorship: 'I feel it would destroy the very essence of what it is.'

So how much time does it take to organise two major community events a year? It may have been the final straw for his first marriage, but he has 'never dared to add it up – because I know it's a lot'. Keith is happy to give advice to other local initiatives although he doesn't have much to do with the voluntary sector in Hastings. Does he see himself as a micro social enterprise? He pauses to think. 'Hmm, I quite like the term – it gives me a label at last'.

Interview with Alex MacGillivray, Hastings, May 1999

Getting the recognition

Many reports note the importance of giving MSEs the recognition they deserve, but go silent on how this can be done. This should be one of those fine things in life that is easier done than said. Here is Keith Leech, who was recently awarded the Order of 1066 in Hastings: 'My name is now on the town hall wall for posterity for outstanding work in the community. I am humbled and proud and feel it is a lovely post script to the piece you have written. I have been recognised!'.

Unfortunately, a more normal experience from our interviews is likely to be being wrapped in red tape, fighting off the attempts of others to take the limelight. Alan Cross has experienced plenty of that.

99% perspiration: Arts in Motion, Birmingham

Just what turns an idea into action? What provides that spark that makes a micro social enterprise determined that they 'can do it'? For P.E. teacher Alan Cross the moment came when he was covering a primary school maths group for an absent colleague. Managing with some difficulty to keep the group working, he looked out of the window and saw a newly qualified teacher with a maths specialism struggling to teach a group of 11-year-olds football. Alan thought 'Why am I here and why is she there? Why aren't we organising primary education better?'

Alan set up Arts in Motion, reflecting his interest in jazz as well as in sport. Working in a small inner city secondary school, his football coaching was so effective that scouts from League Clubs were regular visitors to school matches. When the school was finally closed, he followed his "can do" instincts and launched the concept of specialist teachers in sport and music being contracted to a range of inner city primary schools.

It's hard work, though. Alan's dream is to re-organise primary school staffing by having a smaller group of generalist teachers providing stability and the feeling of family that the best primary schools have. A range of peripatetic can do experts in different subjects, music, sport, drama, perhaps history and geography would support these core staff. Not all school advisers in the Local Education Authority agree, arguing that it would be better for all primary teachers to deliver the basics in all subjects.

Alan has contracts with two primary schools so far and has to sign on to try and make ends meet whilst he tests out whether the enterprise will work. He has glowing references from the people he has worked with. 'Can doers' want to change things; they can make bureaucrats uncomfortable. Alan Cross has a vision of bringing excellence to primary schools in small doses. He wants to link up social enterprises with primary schools to enrich the education of the children in every way. Some people might do so through contracts to run before and after school clubs. Others, like Alan, would use his specialist skills to start the process of developing sporting excellence where it should start, at the beginning.

Interview with Chris Wadhams, August 1999

What does the future hold for MSEs like the Bonfire Society and for Arts in Motion? It's impossible to say. Will they carry on as they are; run out of steam; or get inspired to go even higher?

Keeping it going

The story below shows what is possible with determination. Sustainable Strength is no MSE, but this Birmingham Settlement project has come up against every type of barrier for low income inner city women with children to return to work, take up a training course or become active in their community. Loss of benefit, lack of availability of affordable childcare, and debt problems incurred as a result of the transition to New Deal options have all been encountered. If MSEs can learn how to overcome these obstacles, too, then the sky is the limit.

High Fliers: Jane Skinner and Sustainable Strength

Jane Skinner quit her job as Assistant Director of Social Services in Birmingham to take up a lower paid and less secure post as chief executive of Birmingham Settlement in 1989. She had worked for many years as a community development worker and relished the challenge of getting close to grass roots action again. The Settlement's long history of voluntary innovation, she hoped, would give her a go at breaking the tired practice of existing community outreach work. Jane's career change certainly made a difference.

In her five years at the Settlement before she was tragically struck down by cancer, Jane tried to turn its work inside out. She positioned the Settlement to develop new services like Business Debtline to rescue micro-enterprises, fostered the development of research and development links with the University of Birmingham, and developed the first joint voluntary sector – community sector-led SRB partnership in the country. She also backed the Aston Reinvestment Trust in 1995 – the first mutually owned, citywide community loan fund in the UK.

Jane's pet project, though, was 'Sustainable Strength'. She had been a founder previously of the Birmingham Women's Enterprise Development Agency, which after several good years of service she saw lose its way and ultimately fail when it was unable to qualify for support under the tough

---

'contract culture' and output numbers game of the Business Link regime.

Jane took exception to the macho culture of Business Link and railed against its stereotype of yuppie entrepreneurs oriented to making loads of money. She insisted that fast growth enterprise was the rare exception. Small, slow growth enterprise was the norm out there, struggling in the inner city. The flash suits were simply ignorant of the real needs and how to support and foster them. To Jane, it was not so much about money, but principally about fostering joint entrepreneurship through mutual aid groups.

Unable to secure much help from Business Link, Jane and colleague Jane Slowey began to test out the model of community entrepreneurship in 1994. Before her death in 1997, Jane had motivated a small group of women at Birmingham Settlement to complete a successful pilot phase. The project was launched in June 1998 by Sheela Patel (see above).

Sustainable Strength is now led by Rumena Ahmed and Pam Burton. While still small, it is developing nicely as a mutual aid service for supporting women's economic empowerment in diverse ways of working together through peer groups. The project is based on a careful analysis of needs and visions that enable women to decide what they would like to do. This may be further education, local project development, self-employment, co-operative development or simply the chance to stay in the self-help group for social solidarity reasons. In just one year, the project has helped launch an interpreting co-operative and a textile co-operative – both enterprises developed by Sylheti and Mirpuri Women. The project has also worked with the University of Birmingham to analyse the barriers in the welfare system for low income women.

Source: Pat Conaty and Birmingham Settlement

Benefit of the doubt

Especially for women, choosing the self-employment route throws up huge barriers to economic independence. This option – which the Government did not originally plan for – is not well recognised by New Deal administrators. To make matters worse, previous support packages for the self-employed that were popular in the early 1990s like the Enterprise Allowance Scheme are no longer available.

'There is a problem about first starting up a business and claiming benefits', says Sustainable Strength. 'It is very difficult... quite often people who have started a business have used up all their funds to set up the business and perhaps there is a one or two month gap where they have no income from the business yet, and they are excluded from benefits'. The report on Sustainable Strength (Davis, Betteridge, Burton and Marsh, 1999), gives numerous other examples of the 'benefits trap' that women run into.

Help is at hand with some local voluntary organisations. The Business Debtline service at Birmingham Settlement is working closely with Sustainable Strength to find solutions to a number of problems faced by micro-social entrepreneurs negotiating the 'benefits maze'. It is also good news that the government is now addressing the need for volunteers to claim modest expenses, reviewing the infamous '48 hour rule', and starting to recognise that participating in certain local exchange schemes should not affect benefits entitlements.

But given how common experiences of the benefits trap seem to be, it is not surprising that many community groups have a more radical critique of the whole benefits system (see box opposite).

So, in the fullness of time, perhaps it is not so unthinkable that social entrepreneurs and informal group activists will be eligible for a participation income. But in the meantime, how can they cope with their resourcing difficulties?

Thinking the unfundable? from Dole to New Deal to Citizenship Income

Fifty years after Beveridge, a debate about an entirely new social security system is beginning to get underway. Accepting that the New Deal has delivered some successes, Hirsch (1999) and Parker (1998) both question its assumptions. Hirsch highlights the five million non-retired adults without jobs; Parker questions the outdated prejudice for work within the private sector and draws attention to the hopes of the inspirers of the welfare state, like William Morris, Ruskin, Hobhouse and Tawney for this necessary toil to give way to socially useful livelihoods.

Parker also observes that the concept of a Family Allowance (now Child Benefit) was developed by Hobhouse in 1911 on the principle of a citizen income for parenthood. As Hobhouse expressed it, such 'payment should be regarded not as a dole, but as recompense for such civic service to enable women to bring up children in health and happiness with no degradation attached to receiving public money.'

Recent promising work to redesign the welfare state pioneered by the late James Meade (1993) and built upon by Atkinson and Sutherland (1995) and Carey Oppenheim (1999) indicates that there may still be scope for the introduction of a new form of 'participation or citizen's income' to support those involved as active citizens working for the common good. Atkinson and Sutherland's model shows that at a flat rate of £20 per week, income to the lowest 10 per cent of households can be raised by 31 per cent.

Oppenheim, who moved from think tank IPPR to the Prime Minister's Policy Unit, highlighted the additional financial and social benefits for the bottom 30 per cent of the population. This led to discussion with the Scarman Trust on the possibility of trialing a 'participation income' in Brighton and Birmingham. Another complementary idea – 'Citizenship Credits' – is being promoted by the National Centre for Volunteering, whereby national insurance contributions could be awarded for active citizenship.

A little further from the current policy agenda is the work of radical new economist James Robertson for a comprehensive Citizen's Income funded by the replacement of the existing system that taxes enterprise and 'work rather than waste' by a new system based on ecological and land taxes.

Source: Pat Conaty

RESOURCES

Low flying heroes will often know how to assemble resources from the most unlikely places, and make them go a long way. By resources, we don't just mean money, which is not the only – or even the most important – resource that most MSEs talked about. Social enterprises like Hastings' Jack in the Green have been extremely reluctant to accept financial support; the shoestring has become a way of life for some MSEs and they are none the worse for it.

Three basic issues emerge from discussions with low flying heroes.

Firstly, they are economical. They can achieve a lot for sums of money that are very modest from most funders' perspectives: the average annual income of 173 community groups in Ashby-de-la-Zouch was reported to be just £180[25]. MSEs are often excellent at mobilising non-financial resources: in kind contributions; a friendly office-worker giving access to out-of-hours photocopying and meeting space; time given by volunteers; media coverage; the list goes on.

These resources enable them to punch way beyond their weight, but tend not to be taken into account when projects are evaluated, or applications are made for follow-up funding. The result can be great frustration when resources are withheld or channelled inappropriately: one local authority officer's salary bill for six months (£20,000) would make the world of difference for Kamara, opposite.

The second important factor is that the standard support package – a one-off grant – must be much more flexible than at present. Several MSEs commented that they felt rushed into spending grants all at once and before they knew exactly what they needed. Some Millennium Partners have acted as buffers, nobly absorbing bureaucratic pressure from above in order to give their grantees more room for manoeuvre. On the other hand, some grants almost seem to have been designed to steer people towards going straight out and buying computing equipment, whether they really need it or not.

Candid Kamara, Birmingham

If you believe the colour supplements, Britain is full of people who say they want to pack up their safe city jobs and go and grow vegetables in the wild and windy Wiltshire countryside. They rarely do.

Micro social enterprises are set up by people whose dreams and ambitions drive them on to take risks most of us would think impossible. Their successes make life in many tough aspects of society that bit more rewarding.

Sue spent over ten years working in a travel agents office. Tina found criminal law fascinating and was training to be a solicitor. Then Sue's company was taken over and Tina found herself doing more routine conveyancing than the legal work she enjoyed the most.

Independently, both women decided to follow their inspiration and look for work in the media. Both found their way to the same training agency specialising in seeking opportunities for women with such ambitions. Both became successful, working as sound recordists and as camera crew on a number of well known pictures.

Tina and Sue found a common interest in using their media skills to publicise the stories of people whose experiences might otherwise be ignored and groups whose needs might otherwise not be met. Together they established Kamara, a micro media enterprise. Camara is an African phrase meaning 'one who teaches from experience'.

'African Woman' is one of Kamara's main ambitious media programmes. In one project Tina and Sue trained a number of women to make a video documenting their experience of coming to Britain from the West Indies. What made the video exceptional was that the women chose to illustrate their experiences by describing the gradual spread of West Indian foods from specialist shops to the everyday shelves of our major supermarkets. 'Projekt' is a multi-media 'summer school' experiment in linking video, dance, theatre and performance poetry with the dreams and frustrations of young people.

The wonder of Kamara is not that they need so much but that they can operate on so little. Local authorities tend to be conservative in their approach to media companies, often hiring the big and expensive rather than the smaller innovative outfits. Tina and Sue have to hire the equipment they need for each contract they do. Just £20k would set the business up with its own equipment and an adequate administrative base.

What Kamara does is important. It brings some of the magic associated with the media to situations that record and celebrate the achievements of individuals who would describe themselves as ordinary. In doing so, it offers opportunities to weave the performing arts, poetry, video and theatre into the lives of people who then find themselves capable of extraordinary achievements.

Interview with Chris Wadhams, August 1999

But, thirdly, not all MSEs are committed to resourcing themselves by the voluntary sector, not-for-profit route. Some groups actually seem to prefer loans rather than grants, although this may seem counter-intuitive, given the presumed desire to evade funding from any tied source to avoid complications and liability. Our back-of-the-envelope analysis suggests that some 15 out of a sample of 100 award winners looked to be heading towards trading activity. Anecdotal evidence from Scotland also confirms that a minority, but a significant one, of community enterprises are interested in loans not grants. Community Enterprise Ltd run a grants and loans programme from the same £90,000 pot of money. Since beginning operation in April 1999, they have had 14 grant applications, and have made six awards for a total value of £7,216. Over the same period they received two loan applications for £5,000 each. Both of these were awarded.[26] Clearly, loan funding deserves more attention as an option for MSEs.

Having no discernible income doesn't necessarily mean a commitment to not making a profit in future. Not all MSEs can or want to become registered charities or constituted bodies, and so look at the bureaucratic prescriptions of current grant application forms with bewilderment, if not downright suspicion. A good example is Fifth Element, in Hastings (see box opposite).

Funding forms are usually alienating, especially if they arrive unsolicited on the doorstep as soon as someone has received a bit of positive media coverage. Policy-makers accept in principle that all departments of government streamline and converge their application forms – a great idea so long as the new forms take into account low levels of functional literacy among a quarter of UK adults, make allowance for chaotic lifestyles, and don't descend into the 'highest common denominator syndrome' of joined up thinking: bringing all the bureaucratic idiosyncrasies of each department together into a single 'monster form'!

Lessons from the formal voluntary sector

Micro social enterprise is about both spotting a need and either seizing a new market opportunity quickly and professionally, or finding a way of

---

In her element: Sharon Burke and Fifth Element, Hastings

When part-time driving instructor Sharon Burke drifted into staging some of the loudest rave parties in Hastings five years ago, she little suspected she was on her way to setting up Fifth Element, a project for lads who were 'socially excluded' but brilliant dance music mixers all the same.

Sharon and her team of street-wise DJs won a Scarman Trust award early in 1999, the first money they had ever received apart from slim takings on the door which would sometimes net a profit, sometimes a loss. There was initially some doubt about whether they would even get the award: this is one social enterprise that doesn't fit neatly into any of the usual categories. Nor does it have all that many fans in the local constabulary.

Despite this, perhaps because of it, the project became increasingly successful. A team of anything between half a dozen and 20 talented DJs were soon playing music to an under 18s Club Night and a series of popular raves on Hastings Pier. The only rule is: "no drugs"; Fifth Element is strict about this. As famous DJs queue up to play with Fifth Element, career opportunities begin to open up for some of the DJs. They then begin to act as inspiration for young people in Hastings, who are more comfortable looking to London for role models.

Sharon's eventual ambition is to use her skills as a driving instructor to teach some of the young DJs to drive, saving her some of the many miles of driving that comes with being a music impresario. The other feature of an outfit like Fifth Element is its 'attitude': essential to be a success in dance music but hopeless for prissy voluntary sector funders. Sharon was sent an application form for further grant aid, asking about constitutions, minutes of agms and so on. 'We don't have a constitution; we don't need a constitution. I doubt we'll ever have a constitution'.

Interview with Alex MacGillivray, September 1999

---

designing a resourcing framework based on a mixture of several different sources of income to make the service enterprise work. Social enterprise requires 'soft-heartedness and hard-headedness'. It unites the passion for social justice with the street sense of small business nous.

Housing associations, urged on by government, have been diversifying into Housing Plus since the mid-1990s. This addition to housing provision can include tenant participation services, training for work through the New Deal and, in the case of 1066 Housing Association in Hastings, community credit union development.

High Fliers: Friendship Housing and Care

When the Griffiths Report introduced 'Care in the Community' in the early 1990s, Susanna McCorry was a computer systems manager for a successful care organisation in Birmingham for the disabled. Friendship Housing Association had a small care service that they wanted to expand. Susanna applied for the manager vacancy for the challenge of the task. She took on her job in 1993; today Friendship Care Choices is one of the most successful social enterprises in the country providing care.

As a result of a sound and hard-headed business strategy, Friendship Care Choices has grown its social business at a rate of over 20 per cent a year and created over 500 permanent salaried jobs, plus a further 100 temporary jobs. All staff are thoroughly trained, pay levels higher than average and hard work on systems and quality has secured Investors in People and many other standards. The volunteering and training opportunities have developed many pathways for Friendship tenants motivated to become carers to secure employment and Friendship Care Choices, after only five years, has developed a business turnover larger than its long established middle-sized Housing Association parent.

Friendship Care Choices evaluates the quality of its services independently through service user groups. It provides services for women, those with learning difficulties, mental health users and black elders. In 1998, Friendship Care Choices won the 1998 National Housing Award for best black and ethnic minority housing policy.

The social enterprise has seven major streams of income and, as many payments are only received considerably in arrears, they have needed to use effectively the broad asset base of the Housing Association to help with cash flow management. Today, after only six years of focussed development, Friendship Care Choices is a successful social enterprise that has created hundreds of inner city jobs and offers domiciliary care services, day centre services, respite care, meals services, 24 hour residential care accommodation as well as a welfare rights advocacy service to assist the vulnerable to claim their benefit entitlements.

Interviewed by Pat Conaty, September 1997

One of the most successful housing associations practising Housing Plus in the Midlands, if not the country, is Friendship Housing and Care in Birmingham (see box above). Friendship Housing and Care by no means fits our definition of an MSE, but Susanna's canny sense of how to seize an opportunity when it arises and pursue it with focus and single-minded determination to succeed provides useful lessons to MSEs that want to make it into the big league.

Too grand for us?

There is potentially quite a bit of money around for MSEs. A total of £200 million has been made available for the Millennium Awards, much of which is to be distributed in small grants to grassroots schemes. By mid-2000, some 12,000 awards had been made, with, potentially, nearly 30,000 still remaining, while unLTD should be able to make over 1,000 awards a year for long into the future. This kitty could go a long way towards supporting deserving MSEs in the most deprived neighbourhoods – and elsewhere too.

More money will undoubtedly be needed if the government is to see community activity double or treble, but the sums will not be astronomical. Remember that in Ashby-de-la-Zouch, the average income of community groups was just £180 a year. The Ore Valley Forum in Hastings, co-ordinated by Bev Winchester, managed to spend all of £1,000 in five years. Many MSEs have zero income. Of our estimates of total numbers are correct, a fully-fledged national programme could cost less than £100m a year.

Even given enough money, how should it be distributed? Standard grants run to thousands of pounds, but is this the right amount, at the right time? Probably not: spending such a comparatively large, one-off sum of money in a hurry seems to have been a disruptive experience for MSEs.

Some MSEs said they would have preferred more time to identify what need to meet, and more time to spend what they had. One cynic even wondered whether the timing of awards runs more according to the availability of the local VIPs at launch ceremonies and the accounting needs of financial years in Whitehall than the real lifecycles of the MSEs.

The Scarman Trust and Millennium Commission: flexible red tape?

The Scarman Trust was successful in applying to the Millennium Commission in 1997, winning a grant of £1.2 million, topped up by £100,000 from NatWest Bank to give grants to 450 community activists involved in new grassroots initiatives.

While the scheme has been very successful on the ground, the paperwork has not been easy for the Scarman Trust. Director Matthew Pike soon saw the need to erect 'administrative firewalls' between MSEs and national funding bodies. He found that £2,000 was the smallest award allowed by the Millennium Commission, and that the money had to be spent in six months. While Can Do applicants benefited from a very simple application form, the Scarman Trust itself was then expected to submit very detailed reports and asset registers for award winners.

Naomi Alexander, supporting the Can Do awards in Sussex, actively encouraged award winners not just to rush out and buy a computer and printer with their £2,000 cheque.[27] A future alternative could be the possibility of stepped awards, an idea borrowed from micro-business support in the South and the USA, where successful use of a small sum makes an MSE eligible for a larger one.

This buffering role is a model of what the formal voluntary sector can do to support MSEs, but it cannot be taken for granted. Not all that many charities have been prepared to battle it out with Millennium Commission auditors on principles of public value for money. It remains to be seen how successful the new unLTD coalition can be in keeping up the fight against red tape

Interview with Matthew Pike, Scarman Trust, November 1999

So what do MSEs want to spend money on, when they get it? Here is a rough assessment, based on what 96 Scarman Trust Can Doers planned to spend their awards on. In descending order of priority:

- equipment (non-computer)
- space needs (eg rent or costs to convert)
- materials (eg stationery, art materials, food)
- professional fees (eg trainers, facilitators, advisers)
- printing

- training course costs

- transport costs (eg for senior citizens, children, the disabled)

- computer equipment and software

- volunteer expenses

- childcare costs

It would be useful to look more carefully at spending patterns, because a number of the things on this list could equally well be swapped or rented rather than purchased. Local exchange trading schemes (LETS) and Time Banks, which enable cash-strapped MSEs to trade among themselves, are not just for aromatherapy and plumbing among the middle classes.[28]

Recognition and media coverage

Media coverage is not on the shopping list, but can be a resource worth its weight in gold. Fifth Element raised its profile massively by persuading local TV station Meridian to cover one of its events as a news story – this took a little ingenuity, according to Sharon Burke. Another Hastings Can Doer, Sebastian from film-making co-op Magic Friends, also has a good sense of how to exploit the media interest in his work. Media coverage lifts morale, boosts recognition, gives free advertising, builds networks and can provide some protection from hostile take-overs.

Local dynamo Sue Johnson, with friends Joan and Bob Reed, set up the first credit union in Hastings and St Leonards, and won a Can Do award for her efforts. She has become extremely frustrated by the reluctance of the council and local newspaper to celebrate the amazing fact that nine different groups won Can Do awards in Hastings: surely a record for a town of 80,000.

'The problem', says Sue , 'is getting known and recognised. There are lots of people doing things in this community, but they're not known about because they're not pushy. Other people do a couple of things and everyone has to know about it!' Sue reckons the solution could be a local bulletin, maybe coming out quarterly and listing the work of all the 'unsung heroes'. This would certainly capture the attention of the local bureaucrats – and even perhaps net groups some extra resources. 'Who knows', she says, 'a local businessman might think: oh, I've got a few hundred …'

Training and materials

Money and fame alone don't guarantee success. In fact, unless other support is given too, they can do just the opposite. Yet such support packages are few and far between.

Community Links, a Newham-based voluntary organisation, started monitoring the support it was giving to other local groups, especially in the area of fundraising. It found that many groups were either unsuccessful in the bids they went on to submit, collapsed as a result of not being able to manage the result, or simply wandered away.

As Michael Pitchford, development worker at Community Links, put it: 'Links was faced with a choice: either stop offering support altogether, or do it properly'.[29] They decided on the latter, and set up the First Steps programme in 1995 to provide a two-year schedule of training and tailored support that values good practice and builds upon success.

But it is important to recognise that not all MSEs will embrace training opportunities. Fred Rattley points out that some will 'fear they will be turned into something they do not want to be'. Some groups are so locally focused and caught up in their own project that they are too busy to see the value in networking.

Two other welcome initiatives were announced in late 1999 by the Home Office to tackle social exclusion at the grass roots. Over three years, £1 million will go towards a training fund for individuals and community groups to exchange ideas with other 'social entrepreneurs'. What still needs to be clarified is how such 'horizontal support networks' can be set up in practice. This will need careful planning.

A new community resource fund will also provide grants of up to £500 for small groups which have failed to secure other funding; a sort of runners' up prize. The money could be used for anything from a pensioner's day trip to resources for a residents group, and the paperwork should be light.

Other innovative resources are becoming available to MSEs. Examples include a computer database on tried and tested community regeneration ideas and techniques, based on John F C Turner and Renate Reuther Greaves's work now being developed at the Hastings Trust. Another is a fact bank of bright ideas on colour-coded cards developed by Tony Gibson at the Neighbourhood Initiatives Foundation. A third is the web site known as the participation cook book being developed by Perry Walker at New Economics Foundation. MSEs are always eager for such easy-to-use information on what has worked (and not worked) elsewhere.

Workspace and social enterprise incubators

Many MSEs may thrive as kitchen table operations, but for some of them, sooner or later the issue of premises comes up. It may be because people get tired of having their living rooms become campaign offices, or because the group finally exhausts a host charity's hospitality, or because there's no longer enough room and a bigger meeting venue has to be hired by the hour. Eventually, many community self help groups which are on a growth path begin to talk about leaving home and getting their own place. Kevin Carias, who edits the Hastings environmental newsletter *Here and Now*, said of his move into an office at Hastings Trust, 'it's nice to have an office: my front room is choked with papers and a monstrous computer screen!'.

Many MSEs identify workspace as a headache: finding affordable and effective premises can be a difficult process. Fifth Element has a small office cum recording studio on Hastings Pier, which, says Sharon Burke, has been very important for raising their profile (or at least had, because at the time of writing, Hastings Pier has just gone into bankruptcy and closed). OASIS, a local advice, support and information service, has benefited from being given fine premises by 1066 Housing Association on the Ore Valley Estate.

Much recent attention has been given to the desirability of helping voluntary groups to take ownership of lucrative assets, typically in the form of property. Well-known groups like Coin Street and the North Kensington Amenity Trust were very lucky to be given extremely lucrative assets in this way. But for the vast majority of MSEs, becoming a development trust with its own revenue-generating property is just not an option.

There is still a role here for other organisations to help. Managed workspace has long been popular for micro-businesses, and is now taking off for micro-social enterprise. The most successful examples take an active interest in all aspects of their tenants' development.

The Custard Factory in Digbeth, Birmingham, has helped incubate over 200 micro-enterprises and small organisations in its time. Benny Gray, the ex-journalist developer of the Custard Factory has opened another convivial workspace property, The Big Peg in Birmingham's Jewellery Quarter that has been equally successful. Bootstrap Enterprises, in Hackney, London, started off in the late 1970s as a TV repair service. It now develops projects and businesses creating local jobs and training opportunities. Examples include a vegetarian café, a paper recycling business and a managed workspace enterprise providing 180 jobs.[30]

Such landlords act as social enterprise 'incubators'. More research is needed on how these incubators function so effectively without smothering their charges, which is always a danger. The idea of making whole neighbourhoods social enterprise zones, as recently suggested by David Robinson and colleagues, also looks promising. The question is how to match up such initiatives with the need that most MSEs have to be right on the doorstep: for example on the Ore Valley estate on the outskirts of Hastings, not in the Old Town where the nice premises are available.

It is also high time that local government, schools, businesses, large voluntary groups and even central government departments woke up and realised that their own luxuriously-appointed (by MSE standards) premises are usually empty for hours on end when MSEs are at their most active – in the evenings and at weekends. An open door policy could go far to help meet needs.

Getting accountability under control

One of the big concerns of public and business sectors wanting to fund the MSEs is accountability. Although the sums involved are individually small, in aggregate they may well be large enough to warrant such concern. Even so, the real scandal is the resources devoted to ensuring accountability. It is commonplace for 10–15 per cent of total project funding to be spent on monitoring and evaluation, and there are stories like the rigorous independent evaluation of a community visioning project in Bristol, which cost considerably more than the project itself.[31]

Low flying heroes face the extreme reluctance of Parliament, ministers, government departments and public and charitable funders to take risks with public money, even where very small sums are involved. Activists looking at the Millennium Dome and Royal Opera House might well ask whether this risk aversion is focused disproportionately on the smallest grants. Either way, the cumbersome bureaucratic machine that is rolled out to ensure fiscal accountability may be tolerable for large grant recipients, but unfortunately, it can be a nightmare for small ones. If micro-businesses can obtain start-up grants from Business Link without lots of red tape, then why shouldn't micro-groups get the same treatment? This is a seriously uneven playing field.

Innovation is desperately needed to devise more appropriate forms of accountability. For a start, all public funders should reach agreement so that checks undertaken by one body into financial and management performance would count for other funders.

But there must also be a role for new performance and accountability mechanisms that are not only streamlined but also leave a lasting benefit on the audited group. One is the PQASSO quality system, suitable for pretty small voluntary organisations like Friends United Network.[32] New Economics Foundation has also developed a 'social audit' for small organisations that enables them to demonstrate performance while learning and building capacity. The box overleaf shows how the method has been used by one community enterprise, Play on Wheels.

Some groups will understandably see the accountability agenda as an implied criticism, even as a threat. As Audrey Bronstein of Oxfam points out, there are probably plenty of groups undertaking activities that do not merit public funding or support (and some are plain illegal, like badger baiting clubs). Until we have a better analysis of who, what, where,

Play on Wheels: social accounting on a shoestring

Play on Wheels (PoW) is based in the Pilton area of North Edinburgh. It runs a converted double-decker bus, which provides a mobile crèche service throughout the area. It aims to assist local women access training courses, to create (part-time) work for local people and to be a good employer. It also seeks to be effectively community owned and controlled and to campaign generally for improved childcare provision and standards.

PoW employs three permanent part-time staff and a core group of nine sessional crèche workers with up to 20 others on the books. The first social audit year ran from November 1993 to October 1994 and PoW decided to continue with its social book-keeping, even though resources were very tight. The social audit was arranged and sponsored by Community Enterprise Lothian. Key points of the social audit process included:

- improved attendance records at crèches.

- the introduction of worker record sheets and training record sheets.

- the inclusion of regular social audit items on the agenda of monthly management committee meetings.

- quarterly discussions with the social audit consultant.

- quarterly inspections by the social audit consultant of the social book-keeping records and an analysis of usage, training and employment.

- year-end questionnaire and discussion with some users and sessional workers.

- year-end discussion with permanent workers.

- an 'objectives questionnaire' for management committee members and also an 'impact' group of community leaders, followed up by telephone interviews.

Some of the key points, which arose from the social audit for PoW to consider, were:

- the importance of marketing their service more aggressively so as to better meet the key objectives of helping women access training and job creation.

- the need to target other venues and clients during the 'close' season for training courses.

- how to build on the undoubted PoW success in re-introducing long-term unemployed women to training and to the labour market.

- the importance of being able to distinguish in the social book-keeping records between regular and occasional users.

- the importance of an ongoing in-service training programme for all workers (and for the Management Committee).

- how to increase greater participation in the direction of the enterprise by sessional workers and by community members.

PoW has used information from the social audit to back up its application for public sector grant support and to meet the assessment and monitoring needs of the local authority and the Scottish Office. 'It assisted us in evaluating all areas of our work', they reported, 'and gave us a clear picture of the benefit of our service both within Greater Pilton and throughout Lothian.'

Source: John Pearce, in
Social Auditing for Voluntary Organisations, *1996*

the most that can be said is that those already in receipt of public funds should benefit from a system of accountability which is more focused on their own needs.

But even deserving groups may be wary. Similarly, for the smallest outfits, a full social audit will not be practicable. Innovative forms of peer audit and joint accountability among a cluster of groups in a given locality could help. Social audit 'clubs' of, say, a dozen enterprises, with a reputable coordinator such as a religious leader, would be encouraged to help audit each other in a streamlined and constructive fashion. This could take the form of a consistent (and verifiable if necessary) set of measurements of the amount of social capital created by local projects.

Annabel Jackson, who evaluated the first 12,000 Millennium Awards in 2000, found that the average project attracted 1,000 hours of volunteer time. Conservatively valued at the minimum wage, these contributions by local people far outweigh the financial contributions of funders. If a project has attracted no criticism from local 'sweat equity watchdogs', you can be sure that Whitehall bureaucrats won't find any wrong-doing.

So a simple system of time based accounting may be the best form of accountability for small grant projects.

With these and other solutions, the goal must be to minimise the resources diverted into accountability, and make sure that those resources help to develop not demotivate the MSE.

As Sheela Patel rightly pointed out, accountability for MSEs should be primarily to their communities, not to outside bodies. It is to these relationships that we now turn, as the final ingredient of MSE success.

RELATIONSHIPS

Some MSEs are undoubtedly set up by a lone social entrepreneur, working away in splendid isolation against all odds until hey presto, a breakthrough is made. But teamwork is an essential feature of most MSEs, whether they are dynamic duos with different and complementary skills, or a group of half a dozen or more like-minded people sharing ideas and energy.

Some of the most successful micro social enterprises are a partnership between people in different walks of life, or between amateurs and professionals working together locally. Resources not available to the individual begin to become available to enterprising networks with things in common. To use the new jargon, this is 'social capital' – the glue that holds society together.

Green fingers crossed:
Jackie & Clare, Ore Valley, Hastings

Jackie Gaunt is a well-known 'serial entrepreneur' on the Ore Valley Estate. She is treasurer of the Ore Valley Forum, involved in parent-teacher activities, working on a cookery book and an oral history project, and trying to set up a community launderette. 'I've been involved in community work for 15 years', she says. 'I think I've probably done my apprenticeship'.

Newest on the list of projects is one that she has been working on closely with Clare Croft, co-ordinator of the Ore Valley estate's popular advice and training centre Oasis. Both experts at getting 'an awful lot going with very little money', they felt sure they were on to a good thing when they applied for funding to reclaim a derelict garden surrounding one of the free standing buildings on the estate.

Sure enough, a £1,000 grant soon arrived, and the first step was to chop down the weeds. 'It looks much bigger now its been mowed', says Jackie, chastened for a moment by the ambitious project.

Ten women have got involved so far; four had never done anything else on the estate. This brings with it a growing network of resources: Chris and

Donna both just so happen to be married to landscape gardeners; Nigel from the council will donate bulbs, a water butt and compost bin; 1066 has given the land; a tutor from the University of Sussex has offered a one day course on gardening... Jackie laughs. 'I drag people into things!'.

Where will the project be in five years? Jackie and Clare reel off a list of ideas: a food co-op, a healthy eating club, allotments, catering for local events. So is all this part of a carefully thought-out business plan? 'No, it's organised chaos, really. But one thing's for sure, by the time we're finished, the whole estate will be benefiting from the open space and fresh vegetables'.

Interviewed by Alex MacGillivray, May 1999

The Ore Valley project seems to work well precisely because Jackie and Clare are so different, though since the interview, everything has changed, and Jackie now has Clare's old job! Sometimes, though, success comes not from diversity but from strength in numbers. The case studies above make clear that even MSEs set up by social entrepreneurs like Keith Leech rely on large amounts of teamwork. A dynamic duo like Jackie and Clare does too. But an MSE can just as well be a group of 40, like the Hindu Women's Network (see opposite).

Making up numbers

Just how many local people can MSEs involve, then? Predictably, the experts don't agree. Some believe that, currently, one person in twenty (five per cent) of a typical local neighbourhood may be involved in community activity.[33] Others believe the number is a good deal higher.

Without getting drawn too far into this debate, our case studies suggest that there is no ideal number of participants. The PAT 9 report suggested 'a reasonable target' that the numbers of people involved should treble in five years. In other words, a typical community would see numbers involved increase from 150 people to 450. Not surprisingly, some community groups have expressed concern about the pressure they may come under to 'make up numbers': to involve ever-larger numbers of people in their activities. In principle, such expansion sounds like a good thing, but obviously, growth needs to be handled very carefully, and in some cases may simply not be desirable.

Us and them: Hindu Women's Network, Birmingham

Sheela Patel, the community activist from Bombay, after visiting a number of projects in Britain, remarked on the continuing focus here on the individual. She had noticed that when people feel badly treated by officials, they ring up or call at an office to complain. People feel that 'they' should do something for 'me'. In Bombay, she said, you would first find a number of people suffering the same problem. Then you would go and complain to the official collectively. 'We' would try and work with 'them' to solve the problem.

The Hindu Women's Network uses this collective tradition to challenge other traditions. Its founder, Rama Bharandawa, was frustrated at the way the Hindu Council of Birmingham was dominated by men. She contacted other women who agreed that the contribution that Hindu women could make to society was not properly recognised. Through meeting in each other's houses, the Network became established.

Over 40 women now find the support of the Network valuable. Some are middle class, with professional jobs. They have overcome the barrier of male disapproval of women with careers. Others, in contrast, find the support of the sisterhood important in building confidence and self-esteem. The Network is not wholly social. High profile speakers from the Asian community regularly accept invitations to attend meetings. Tough issues like HIV and Aids are on the agenda, as is the issue of family culture and the demands for greater independence from young people.

The *somaj* is the basic community group structure; each elects its own president. Rama Bharandawa was the first woman president of a somaj. Her election led to some men resigning and others expecting her to fail. She didn't, and her example proved that the Network was a powerful influence in winning equal treatment and respect for women. Other groups now approach the Birmingham Network for speakers at their meetings and groups in London and Leicester are beginning to develop.

The Hindu Women's Network is at the centre of changes in Hindu society. One of its objectives is to combat the divisions that reflect the caste system and bring women from all groups together. Neither is it insular in its approach to other organisations. A recent conference on community enterprise was attended by nearly 100 women. It was organised by the Network in partnership with the Birmingham Training and Enterprise Council and the City's Economic Development Department. Increasingly the Network is consulted by a range of

> statutory and voluntary groups on issues affecting the Hindu community although its members are careful to indicate that their views should be seen as personal rather than representing a formal organisational position.
>
> In most areas of the developing world, and in many areas of Britain, women are the driving forces for changes at local, and increasingly at regional and national level. The stereotype of the subservient Asian woman never was true and the Hindu Women's Network is witness to the important role such organisations could play in encouraging broad based community action.
>
> *Interview with Chris Wadhams, August 1999*

However, for the right groups, if they could learn a few tricks about managing relationships from formal voluntary organisations like the Birmingham Credit Union Movement (another example of a 'high flier'), there is no doubt that some MSEs could go on to mobilise really large numbers of people.

High Fliers: Birmingham Credit Union Movement

Credit unions have grown in Birmingham from only three to 31 in the past twelve years. Mutual savings and investment in the financial co-operatives has grown from £150,000 to over £11 million today and membership citywide is now over 15,000. In 2001/02, Birmingham community credit unions will open their first dedicated shop-front facilities in two areas of the city, with a population of 100,000 each. Shop-front services to be provided include savings and loans, bill payment, insurance, and home improvement finance. At the present growth rate, every district in Birmingham could have access to a local community credit union by 2002.

It all started in 1985. Jim Dearlove was then working from home as a credit union organiser for the Association of British Credit Unions. He teamed up with an unemployed Irish community activist and former bank cashier, Marlene Moore. She was incensed by the lack of savings facilities to those on low income by comparison to Ireland and she was also angry about the sharp practice of high cost moneylenders and the growing rate of bank branch closures in inner city Brum.

With Marlene's passion and retail banking background plus Jim's credit union know-how, they forged the vision of a credit union development plan. As a result of the 'earache' Marlene was giving both City officers and local politicians about the disinvestment issue, Jim was able – diplomatically of course – to persuade the Council to provide resources to recruit a small team to form the Birmingham Credit Union Development Agency (BCUDA), founded in 1987.

For over a decade, the two of them and other BCUDA staff used classic community organising techniques to recruit, train and support mutual aid groups in a growing number of low-income neighbourhoods in order to found the co-operatives and legally register them. It could take as long as two years to get mutual aid groups to the state of skill and preparation as volunteers to meet the Registrar of Friendly Societies' increasingly strict licensing criteria.

The credit union movement's success now draws on the regular weekly involvement of more that 400 volunteers taking in savings, making decisions on loans, recruiting new members, and operating collection points at schools, community centres, and in church halls. The volunteers run most of the community credit unions without any paid staff but are supported by four training and service development workers.

Jim's inspiration comes from the community organising techniques of Saul Alinsky and the liberation theology of Paulo Freire, Ivan Illich, and Joseph Cardign. He had worked as an isolated credit union organiser in the 1980s covering the patch from West Wales to East Anglia, and felt the only realistic way forward was to engage in an intensive organising effort in one city. The aim would be to quickly establish a critical mass of financial co-operatives. He hoped they would feed off each other and catalyse a broad based movement for remutualising financial services for those unable to access conventional banks and building societies.

With this strategy, the Birmingham Credit Union movement is actively rebuilding co-operative enterprise for those on low and moderate income, very much in the spirit of the Rochdale Pioneers. Tragically, though, Marlene died in 1997.

Interviewed by Pat Conaty, September 1999

Horizontal support networks: links with other MSEs

Individual MSEs may be thriving, and often involving surprisingly large numbers of local people. But many interviewees said that they could do with more networking opportunities. The big question is, what can be done to help develop local networks, without swamping them?

Informal networking can also take place when award winners meet up and socialise. For example, Fifth Element in Hastings helped a young film-makers' co-op, Magic Friends, by making some music as a soundtrack for their first ultra-low budget film. It was only when they met by chance in London that Jackie from the Ore Valley, Hastings and Sue and Tina from Kamara in Birmingham discovered an unexpected mutual interest in oral history and cookery. Slightly more formal is the group Green and Away, which, assisted by New Economics Foundation and others, has run a popular annual 'summer camp' for environmental groups that combined training, workshops and informal networking. A similar approach could be adopted for MSEs, perhaps building on the Millennium Commission's Fellowship Scheme.

'Perhaps the most exciting development of the programme', says Matthew Pike of the Scarman Trust, 'is the extent to which Can-Doers are interested in working together on collaborative projects on key issues of widespread concern. Very often, they recognise that small scale projects are not enough.' The Trust is helping to build local alliances, like the group in Birmingham who helped organise a national conference on public health.

New technology is often assumed to be socially excluding, and there is no doubt that some MSEs see the computer as an enemy of local community. But there are beginning to be examples of how it can be just the opposite. One innovative idea is the Social Internet project, Scarman Trust's plan to set up an electronic network for its 450 award-winning Can-Doers, by:-

- equipping Can-Doers with quality refurbished computer hardware, appropriate software, internet access, training and technical support; and

● working with Can-Doers to develop new applications, tools and networks in harmony with existing ways of doing things to help unlock the power of communities and create opportunities for mutual learning.

Another example is the use of information and communication technology (ICT) on run-down estates such as Angell Town, and Manor and Castle (see box).

ICT in Manor and Castle

Information and Communication Technology (ICT) is changing the way we work, communicate, shop and live our lives. It seems like 'the net' is becoming dominated by massive corporations, but ICT may actually help foster small scale organisations such as micro-enterprises and community networks, giving them the possibility to rapidly increase their profile, reach new markets and enhance the dissimulation of information. By working together and engaging in e-commerce, these enterprises can compete with major businesses in their field and exploit niche markets.

Access to information is increasingly the key to any successful organisation, and ICT enables them to make better-informed choices and decisions. The empowering capacity of ICT also allows more people to participate more effectively in information and communication processes.

New ways of working are rapidly being established with the advent of telecentres, virtual offices and organisations. Office space gets replaced by the mobile office – a laptop, modem and mobile phone – saving costs and making geographical location less relevant. These changes could benefit informal and small-scale organisations more than large ones.

Manor and Castle, outside Sheffield, has an official registered unemployment of over 20%; 34% of all households are in receipt of income support; 35% of all families with children are single parent households; 55% of all households with children have no wage earner, and 75% of households have no access to a car.

A deprived area, then, but determined to do something about it. The Manor & Castle Community Information Network has established an area-wide information and electronic mail system. It brings together information and resources from existing training, schools, business, health, housing,

---

environment, childcare, youth and community groups. Some examples of the use of the Information Network:

- The Trust has information and forms to download to local computers needed by organisations for funding bids etc.

- Local businesses and groups are advertising their business and services to the local community, and any job opportunities.

- The SRB Training Forum is providing information on all training opportunities available in the area.

- A local, electronic notice board is available for groups and individuals to advertise events.

Source: Marco Kuntze and New Economics Foundation

Inspired by this example, NEF and others are investigating the possibility of 'wiring up' housing estates so that they can get access to the internet. The idea would be to use Time Banks as a system to record community development work. Clocking up a given number of hours – say 100 – would make groups or individuals eligible for a reconditioned personal computer with web access. Such computers are increasingly being made available as businesses upgrade their equipment.

Not all MSEs will jump at the chance of networking; some are little interested in personal growth or organisational development. Important as it is, they just want to 'get the ****** project finished so they can get on with their lives'. Fair enough.

Harmonious relations with the local powers that be

The local powers-that-be should obviously be supportive and nurturing towards MSEs, whether they are government, local authorities, business, media or the formal voluntary sector. Certainly, our case studies show that MSEs benefit from such support. 'Given the financial demands of funders', says Fred Rattley of the Allens Croft Project, 'our experience with two projects is that they could not manage without the support of a more established organisation'.

If there is an occasional little bit of obstruction, perhaps it is unintentional: like a sow crushing one piglet out of her litter in a crowded sty? The sad reality is that in too many cases, local institutions have it in for MSEs. They can act destructively, whether by crushing or co-opting ideas, resources and reputations. In the regeneration game, the voluntary sector as a whole faces a perverse sort of competition for problem-solving ideas with central government and its agencies, local authorities, MPs, innumerable task forces, and businesses desperate to establish their licence to operate. Powerful institutions are continuously seizing the bright ideas and innovations of the MSEs and claiming the best of the bunch as their own.

Sue Johnson, who helped set up the Hastings and St Leonards Credit Union, resents the attitude of 'professionals insisting that we can't do it without them'. Her experience is familiar to many MSEs. Although she has enjoyed support both from key councillors, social services and from the 1066 housing association, the credit union is also being crowded. The first funded post in the credit union ought to have been good news. In fact, it led to considerable tension: funders and activists fundamentally disagreeing on who the new staff member should report to.

Unfortunately, there is ample evidence that even the established voluntary sector is not averse to muscling in, and plagiarising the good ideas and innovations of community groups. Conversely, it's probably fair to say that some MSEs have become so combative that they don't help their case. Hammersmith & Fulham Council, for example, was getting a bit too much ear-ache from some vociferous groups with questionable credentials. The council recently reviewed the 'representativeness' of the borough's voluntary organisations with a view to streamlining its consultation processes. Compared to the larger, more professionalised bodies, MSEs are likely to do well on two key features: shared characteristics, and interactions. However, there is a risk that the smaller end of the sector will be penalised for not being able to demonstrate hard evidence of its membership base.

What can be done? Compacts are very fashionable these days, and a carefully-drafted compact, or code of good practice, along the lines of the government-formal voluntary sector one, might help protect MSEs from over-attentive institutions. They 'may well be affected, directly or indirectly, by Government legislation, regulation and changes in social policy,' said the Home Office compact on relations between Government and the voluntary and community sector in England, issued in November 1998. The report went on: 'It is important that the distinctive needs and interests of community groups are taken into account as their perspective and concerns may differ from those of other voluntary organisations. A code of good practice will be developed to facilitate and reflect this'. Highlighting bad practice is the stick that could go with this carrot.

And if local institutions were rewarded not by publicity and measurable inputs and outputs, but by the extent to which they could demonstrate real support for community self-help itself, the temptation to bully would be substantially reduced.

It was this adversarial aspect to MSEs' relationships with authority that made us choose the title 'low-flying heroes' for this report. Too often, MSEs are actively trying to keep below the radar and avoid detection as they go about their business. It's amazing how many groups seem able to thrive in this harsh environment. But a more harmonious relationship has to be desirable if local involvement in community activity is to double or treble in the next few years.

CONCLUSIONS AND RECOMMENDATIONS

The micro social enterprises described in this report are incredibly numerous – there are probably 600–900,000 of them. No-one reliably knows if overall numbers are on the rise, or in decline. They are also extremely diverse. Some are struggling; some thriving. Some are on their way to becoming more formal organisations; others have almost finished what they set out to do; still more are happy to carry on as they are.

The lifecycles of the MSEs we studied are complex and challenging, but they are by no means like the life described by 17th century political scientist Thomas Hobbes: 'nasty, brutish and short'. In fact, some positively seem to relish the ducking and diving needed as they deliberately fly below the radar on their missions.

This research drew on a scant literature which largely ignores MSEs, and then twenty interviews, in one English city and one town. Our thanks to Barry Knight and other experts for pointing out, politely, that this is a rather limited 'sample size' on which to draw firm conclusions and make reliable recommendations about approaching a million other MSEs. That is why some of the recommendations sound rather tentative, and why some questions remain unanswered.

These uncertainties should not go unanswered for much longer. The answers will come from a judicious mixture of:

- meticulous further research, both theoretical and applied; and

- getting stuck in with some of the most promising ideas right away to see how they work.

Diversity: recognition and understanding

For once, the case for further research looks genuine. The 'social ecology' of micro-social enterprises needs to be much better understood. Research to advance such understanding must be on a par with the knowledge of small business dynamics within the next few years.

Diversity is the main feature of MSEs, yet there is still too much prejudice, based on stereotypes – and even vested interests within local authorities and the voluntary sector – which see large, formal organisations as the only viable service providers. The serious lack of understanding of whether and how given community initiatives can grow from concept, to experiment, to project, to service and to established body over five to ten years, impedes the development of effective policy and relevant support mechanisms. Conversely, too many expectations can be heaped on informal groups that do not want to or cannot go down the service delivery route.

Government, business, the voluntary sector and academia all need to improve their understanding about and respect for MSEs. Awards schemes, exchanges, in depth study tours, and escapes from the London seminar circuit can all help build the sort of recognition that MSEs value.

There is scope for widespread on-the-ground audits of voluntary activity. Large scale surveys covering visions, ambitions and development plans (such as they are) will show which pathways are most popular. More detailed analysis of actual life histories would show what happens to these plans in reality (ladder versus spectrum thinking).

These surveys should be funded by central/regional/local government, undertaken by local voluntary sector organisations, perhaps making use of volunteer time, and with relevant support from academia to ensure coherence and comparability of findings.

There needs to be more acceptance of a coherent terminology: at present each new report (including this one) feels obliged to invent new terms. Categories of activity need to be agreed, so that we can identify growth areas and gaps.

Financing: beyond 'the cheque's in the post'

This improved understanding will challenge overly-prescriptive support packages. The current 'ladder' mentality runs the risk of force-feeding MSEs; giving them a pulse of one-off income – a nice fat cheque – but no sustainable resourcing strategy. Money is not the one and only form of support needed.

The innovative approaches beginning to emerge from some of the best Millennium Award schemes show how community enterprises can be spotted on the radar screen and given new opportunities through recognition and a very small grant. But the MSEs described in this report were by no means universally satisfied by the experience, and some found it troublesome. In particular, some could have done without the pressure to spend the money so fast, and others are not sure that what they spent it on was really what they needed.

- A system of 'stepped micro-grants' available over a longer period should be developed, with gradually increasing sums, flexible spending schedules and easy re-application and reporting processes. UnLTD and other key funding bodies would take a lead in developing this; local trusts would also need to play a part.

- Moving to a single central government grant application form and process is a great idea; but even more needs to be done to streamline the paperwork involved. For the quarter of the adult population that have literacy troubles with official paperwork, other non-paper formats could be developed (eg videos, audio cassette recordings).

- Grants are not invariably what MSEs want or need. In a significant minority of cases (maybe around one in seven), loans might be more appropriate. Micro-loans for micro-social enterprises could be developed by funding bodies in a similar way to the micro-credit principle and practice of group loans which has proven successful internationally.

- Packages should contain more than cash. There is evidence that a majority of MSEs don't even want external funding, let alone actually need it. But some of these could benefit from appropriate non-financial assistance. Credits or vouchers for MSEs to use as they see fit on a range of capacity-building options are an interesting new development promoted byt eh Active Community Unit.

- Time could be a key part of the funding mix. MSEs for example could draw down time donated by companies (eg project management expertise), brokered by a regional or local Time Bank. And to move forward the grant/loan debate, what about government loans that are repayable in time – on approved community projects?

Networking: knowing a woman who can...

Most of the MSEs interviewed agreed that networking was vital to their success. Many of these networks evolve organically, and some researchers believe that this type of 'social capital' cannot in fact be created by policy interventions, only destroyed. But there is growing evidence that the growth of social capital can be encouraged (*Prove It!*, NEF, 2000).

Horizontal learning networks and co-operative relationships between richer and poorer organisations should be encouraged. These must allow for free experimentation from the 'bottom up', trial and error and learning from failure in the spirit of free social enterprise.

Social internet projects look to be very promising if they can ensure access to the most excluded groups as well as 'early adopters'.

Not all MSEs will see the value of networking; they're 110% committed to achieving a specific objective and don't want to be distracted. Accessible case study material demonstrating how networks can actually help to achieve the task in hand as well as build for the future are needed to win over reluctant networkers.

There is considerable 'pent-up demand' for support materials and facilitated networks produced specifically for low flying heroes (for example by NIF, NEF, Hastings Trust and Scarman Trust). But it will take a long time for these initiatives to cater for large numbers at the current rate of development.

MSEs often want to beg or borrow but end up having to buy. Commodity banks for goods and materials could be developed, along the lines of toy libraries. Many companies, local authorities, schools, TECs and large voluntary organisations would be keen to donate materials through a well organised commodity bank.

Alternative currencies such as LETS and Time Banks could provide some help in encouraging MSEs to exchange goods and services amongst themselves.

Getting organised: the appropriate legal structures

For any informal outfit with the ambition and opportunity to grow into more formal structures, it is vital to get those structures right. The charitable route may not be the right one, or just too time-consuming, unless some form of 'starter pack' or micro-charity status can be devised by the Charity Commission as part of its ongoing review.

New, flexible mutual structures could prove equally useful for some groups. Other structures that deserve consideration are loose-knit informal alliances, industrial and provident societies, co-operatives and social businesses. Above all, these structures should be simple, informal and flexible.

There is a clear need for clear and comprehensive guidance and case studies on all these options, including legal advice. This could be a combined job for the Active Community Unit, Local Government Association, Small Business Service, ICOM and umbrella voluntary bodies. The guidance would need to be tailored to local circumstance and followed up locally.

There may be a role for a new national association, along the lines of the social enterprise network being promoted by Jonathan Bland at SEL. It would advance networking, advocacy, and opportunities to celebrate achievements. If not, this role would need to be taken on more proactively by the raft of existing organisations.

There may even be a need for new legislation to advance the micro-social enterprise sector and the wider social economy. A review of charity law, or a new 'mutuality' law as recommended by Gilmore (1998), might help.

Workspace: out of the front room

Small businesses thrive in clusters, be it surgical instrument makers in Sialcott, Pakistan, or multimedia entrepreneurs around Cardiff. Economic development experts are also talking increasingly about development corridors, where businesses can move into progressively larger (or smaller) premises without undue turmoil.

69

Space is a headache, which is why there is growing interest in providing support in geographical clusters or social enterprise zones, but this is a controversial area, with complex lessons from the work of the Custard Factory in Birmingham, Finsbury Park Business Centre and Clerkenwell Workshops in London, the Ethical Property Company in London and Bristol, and even from unsuccessful ventures like the Robert Tressell Workshops in Hastings.

Established voluntary organisations and small businesses can offer micro-social enterprises space, without patronising them or attaching too many strings. On a one-to-one basis, they should be encouraged to offer them space to rent or share, purchase their services, develop joint ventures, share knowledge, provide training or mentoring, and make available access to equipment and facilities. Legislation may however be needed to unblock schools and local government premises.

More research is needed into the idea of dedicated social enterprise 'incubators' (to use the fashionable term) which nurture MSEs in their formative phase. Central government, local authorities, trusts, businesses and training and enterprise agencies would provide support for such incubators.

This could be done through pilot experiments in, say, half a dozen localities. This enabling role could take the form of a secondary co-operative institution looking out for support, training, networking, marketing, workspace, funding and benefit needs of micro-social enterprises.

The proposed development of a Community Land Trust in Birmingham by Aston Reinvestment Trust could be an interesting way to approach MSEs' workspace needs. The green shoots of the new housing co-operative movement could also be of relevance here. Databases of available space for hire at a low or peppercorn rent can also be developed, as the new London Rebuilding Society intends to do.

A Ministry for Micro Social Enterprise? a new role for government

Support schemes for low flying heroes are flavour of the month, with over 50 schemes now providing support running to millions of pounds a year. But, according to Ed Mayo, "this is like cutting the tape on an array of shiny new bicycles, launched without having built the cycleways and paths they will need if they are to go far".

While many local schemes are admirable, there are no mechanisms to ensure that they learn from each other. On past experience, up to half are likely to fail, and there is no guarantee that government will enable the remaining half to evolve into a national system of support for all social entrepreneurs, fully integrated with the benefits regime and lifelong learning. It is not certain that the new Units will have the clout to make this happen, and many low flying heroes, scarred by run-ins with the benefits system, doubt whether government intervention is desirable, full stop.

Some experts believe that the vast majority of MSEs do not want outside support, and fear that intervention would compromise the independence of these groups. Burns and Taylor, for example, have cautioned against most policy interventions – which they consider are more likely to do more harm than good.

There always lurks the policy option of doing nothing, not even research. Many MSEs are likely to survive, perhaps even thrive, in such a hostile environment. But this report shows that there is likely to be enormous untapped potential in the micro social enterprise sector. The potential of active communities will only be fully realised with active support from central and local government, business and the charities. The best assistance possible is to help create a benign environment for development and to offer, very carefully, indirect help through either self-help or community development agency support that is sensitive to a group's needs.

On this cautious basis, this report concludes that there can – and should – be a significant role for central and local government.

The DTI's Small Business Service will in some ways be a test case for MSEs. If this 'one stop shop' can take on a remit to support for-profit micro-enterprise, then there will be a strong case for a non-profit counterpart. This would be a combined role for the Home Office's Active Community Unit, the DETR's Neighbourhood Renewal Unit, and with substantial input from DfEE.

The social security system does not exactly encourage MSEs. We need a level playing field that gives equal weighting to widening both market and civil society participation as similarly valid opportunities for active citizens. Current moves to reform volunteer expenses and the 48 hour rule will be welcome but a much more thorough-going review is needed if the benefits system is to be converted from an obstacle course to a runway.

The voracious accountability needs of government need to be tamed. Paperwork can be slashed by promoting mutual accountability (through team audits and learning groups); but a true developmental relationship with funders based on trust and respect is also vital.

Careful investigation is needed for the role of a 'participation income' (potentially non-means tested and non-taxable), and how this could evolve over time from an Individual Development Account towards a fully-fledged citizen's income scheme. Tax credits for active citizens could also be attractive solutions. Scarman Trust and others are beginning to consult community activists on such systems.

Local government, the new regional bodies and the economic development agencies will all have to demonstrate that they are willing to back MSEs to the hilt. This will require massive shifts in values and organisational flexibility just at the time that these bodies are struggling to establish their own reputations for effectiveness.

So there it is: a major new framework to support micro social enterprise. Without it, many low flying heroes will continue to make progress against the odds, but many will fail to take off and others will 'crash and burn'. To unleash their full potential, we need to move rapidly from disjointed 'pilot' initiatives to a full-scale national support programme.

ANNEX: INTERVIEW QUESTIONS

Tell us about your project or service. When did it get started? How many people are involved? (Paid/Unpaid)

What motivated you to get started? Why this project rather than another one?

What have you been able to achieve so far?

What are the biggest problems or obstacles that you have experienced? How have these problems affected your personal or family life?

What funding have you been able to raise? What has this enabled you to do?

What extra funding do you most need?

Which of the following best describes your project – voluntary organisation, community business, co-operative, charity, small business, or other?

What has been your greatest source of support?

What training, if any, would be helpful to you?

Have you had any guidance or support from established voluntary organisations? How has this helped you?

Are there any organisations you admire and feel I wish I could achieve what they have done? Which are they?

If you could get mentoring help from such organisations would this be helpful?

What other resource needs do have (e.g. premises, equipment, volunteers, other)?

What attempts are you making to get these resources? Has your local voluntary services council been helpful?

How would you describe the success of your project so far?

What ideas do you have for making your project as independent as possible?

As a small project, what forms of discrimination, if any, have you experienced?

Has your local authority helped you? If not, how could it?

Have you produced a 'business plan' for your project? If not, would this possibly be helpful?

In five years time, what do you think your project will be like?

What benefits do you think it will have accomplished?

How do you measure success at present?

Would a local network of projects like yours be attractive to you? How so?

Do you have any questions you would like to ask me?

REFERENCES

Atkinson, A. B. (1995), *Incomes and the Welfare State*, Cambridge University Press, Cambridge.

Berry, Wendell (1996), *The Unsettling of America*, Sierra Club Books, San Francisco, USA.

Burns, Danny and Taylor, Marilyn (1999), *Mutual Aid and Self-Help: Coping Strategies for Excluded Communities*, Policy Press.

Chanan, Gabriel (1999), *Local Community Involvement – A Handbook for Good Practice*, European Foundation, Dublin, Ireland.

Chanan, Gabriel & West, Alison, (1999), Regeneration and Sustainable Communities, Gabriel Chanan, Alison West with Charlie Garratt & Jayne Humm, Community Development Foundation, 1999.

Claeys, Gregory (1987), *Machinery, Money and the Millennium – from Moral Economy to Socialism, 1815–1860*, Polity Press, Cambridge.

Conaty, Pat & Fisher, Thomas, (1999), *Micro-credit for Micro-enterprise*, New Economics Foundation, London.

Crabtree, Tim, Roberts, Andy & McRobie, George, (1992), *Towards a New Sector: macro-policies for community enterprise*, New Economics Foundation, London.

Daly, Herman E. (1996), *Beyond Growth*, Beacon Press, Boston, USA.

Davis, A., Betteridge, J., Burton, P., and Marsh, S. (1999), Overcoming Barriers to Women's Economic Independence – The Sustainable Strength Project Birmingham, An ENACT Report, University of Birmingham.

Edwards, Charles, (no date), Social Entrepreneurship: a new paradigm for public and non-profit management?, Business Briefing, Open University Business School web site.

Elsdon, Konrad (1998), *Studying Local Voluntary Organisations: purpose, methods & findings*, Community Development Foundation, London.

Elsdon, Konrad *et al.*, (1995), *Voluntary Organisations: citizenship, learning and change*, National Institute of Adult Continuing Education, Leicester.

Freedland, Jonathan, (1999), *Bring Home the Revolution: the case for a British republic*, Fourth Estate, London.

Friendship Care Choices Annual Report 1998, Birmingham.

Fromm, Eric (1981), *To Have or to Be*, Abacus, London.

Gibson, Tony (1998), 'Us and Them – How the pacemakers in governance and civil society see themselves and each other', Background Paper for 'Breaking New Ground' Conference at the British Council in London, 20 April 1998.

Gilmore, Rosalind (1998), *Mutuality for the Twenty-first Century, Centre for the Study of Financial Innovation*, London.

Gray, John (1993), *Beyond the New Right – Markets, Government and the Common Environment*, Routledge, London.

Hems, Les, & Passey, Andrew, (1998), *The UK Voluntary Sector Almanac 1998/99*, NCVO, London.

Henderson, Hazel (1993), *Paradigms in Progress – Life Beyond Economics*, Adamantine Press, London.

Hirsch, Donald (1999), *Welfare Beyond Work – Active Participation in a New Welfare State*, York Publishing Services, York.

Hopkins, Eric (1995), *Working-Class Self Help in Nineteenth-Century England*, UCL Press, London.

Huxley, Aldous (1994), *The Perennial Philosophy*, Flamingo Classic, London.

Illich, Ivan (1981), *Shadow Work*, Marion Boyars Publishers, London.

Illich, Ivan (1996), *Deschooling Society*, Marion Boyars Publishers, London.

Illich, Ivan (1978), *The Right to Useful Unemployment*, Marion Boyars Publishers, London.

Jacobs, Jane (1992), *Systems of Survival – A Dialogue on the Moral Foundations of Commerce and Politics*, Hodder and Stoughton, London.

Johnston, Michael & Jowell, Roger (1999), 'Social capital and the social fabric', in: *British Social Attitudes: the 16th report*, Roger Jowell, John Curtice, Alison Park & Katarina Thomson (eds)., National Centre for Social Research, Ashgate, Aldershot.

Kendall, Jeremy, (1998), *The UK Voluntary (Third) Sector in Comparative Perspective: exceptional growth and transformation*, Jeremy Kendall & Stephen Almond, LSE Personal Social Services Research Unit, CAF, JRF & Johns Hopkins Comparative Nonprofit Sector Project, October 1998

Kendall, Jeremy, (1996), *The Voluntary Sector in the UK*, Jeremy Kendall & Martin Knapp, Manchester University Press.

Knight, Barry, (1993), *The Centris Report*.

Knight, Barry, (1998), *Building Civil Society: current initiatives in voluntary action*, Barry Knight, Cathy Pharaoh *et al.* (eds), CAF.

Knight, Barry and Stokes, Peter (1996), The Deficit in Civil Society in the United Kingdom, Working Paper No. 1, Foundation for Civil Society, Birmingham.

Knight, Barry (1998), 'The Nuts and Bolts of Civil Society: Some Relevant British Experience', Background Paper for 'Breaking New Ground' Conference in London at the British Council, 20 April 1998.

Kropotkin, Peter (1987), *Mutual Aid – A Factor of Evolution*, Freedom Press, London.

Leadbeater, Charles and Christie Ian (1999), *To Our Mutual Advantage*, Demos, London.

Leadbeater, Charles and Martin, Stephen (1998), *The Employee Mutual*, Demos, London.

Mauss, Marcel (1990), *The Gift – the Form and Reason for Exchange in Archaic Societies*, W. W. Norton, London.

Meade, J. E. (1993), *Liberty, Equality and Efficiency*, MacMillan, Basingstoke, Hampshire.

Mill, John Stuart (1994), *Principles of Political Economy and Chapters on Socialism*, Oxford University Press, Oxford.

New Economics Foundation, (1997), *Community Works!*, NEF, London.

Oppenheim, Carey (1999), 'Welfare to Work: Taxes and Benefits' in *Welfare in Working Order*.

Osmond, John (1986), *Work in the Future – Alternatives to Unemployment*, Thorsons Publishing Group, Wellingborough, Northamptonshire.

Parker, Julia (1998), *Citizenship, Work and Welfare*, MacMillan Press, Basingstoke, Hampshire.

Patel, Sheela (1997), *From the Slums of Bombay to the Housing Estates of Britain*, Centre for Innovation in Voluntary Action and Oxfam, London.

Pharaoh, Cathy, (1998) *Dimensions of the Voluntary Sector 1998 edition*, ed Cathy Pharaoh, Matthew Smerdon, CAF.

Polanyi, Karl (1944), *The Great Transformation*, Beacon Press, Boston, USA.

Rifkin, Jeremy (1996), *The End of Work, G. P. Putnam's Sons*, New York, USA.

Robinson, David, Dunn, K. & Ballintyne, S., (1998), *Social Enterprise Zones: building innovation into regeneration*, Joseph Rowntree Foundation, York, 1998.

Rogaly, B., Fisher, T. & Mayo, E., (1999), *Poverty, Social Exclusion and Microfinance in Britain*, Oxfam GB / New Economics Foundation.

Ruskin, John (1985), *Unto This Last and Other Writings*, Penguin, London.

Russell, Bertrand (1997), *Principles of Social Reconstruction*, Routledge, London.

Russell, Bertrand (1985), *Roads to Freedom*, Unwin Paperbacks, London.

Schumacher, E. F. (1980), *Good Work*, Abacus, London.

Seabrook, Jeremy (1990), *The Myth of the Market*, Green Books, Bideford, Devon.

Seabrook, Jeremy (1988), *The Race for Riches*, Green Print, Basingstoke, Hants.

Sutherland, Holly (1997), 'Submission to the Low Pay Commission' Micro-simulation Unit, Cambridge University.

Taylor, Marilyn (2000), *Top Down Meets Bottom Up: neighbourhood management*, Joseph Rowntree Foundation, York.

Thompson, E.P. (1966), *The Making of the English Working Class*, Vintage Books, New York, USA.

Thompson, E.P. (1991), *Customs in Common*, Penguin Books, London.

Wann, Mai (1995), *Building Social Capital*, Institute for Public Policy Research, London.

Williams, Colin C. and Windebank, Jan (1999), *A Helping Hand: harnessing self-help to combat social exclusion*, York Publishing Services, York.

Wilson, J. (1995), *Two Worlds – Self Help Groups and Professionals*, Ventura Press.

Wright, Anthony (1987), R. H. Tawney, Manchester University Press, Manchester.

Zadek, Simon, & Thake, Stephen, (1997), *Practical People, Noble Causes*, New Economics Foundation, London.

END NOTES

1   The so-called PAT 9 report on community self-help is by Policy Action Team 9, a task force assembled by the Social Exclusion Unit at the Cabinet Office. There were 2 other types of group mentioned in their 1999 report: mutual/economic groups and groups based on a community of interest. These are qualitative and don't imply a given level of size or formality. If small and informal, such groups could be MSEs.

2   See for example Michael Johnston and Roger Jowell: 'Social capital and the social fabric', in: *British Social Attitudes: the 16th report*, Roger Jowell, John Curtice, Alison Park & Katarina Thomson (eds)., National Centre for Social Research, Ashgate, Aldershot, 1999.

3   First applied to not-for-profit voluntary organisations by management writer Peter F. Drucker in his books *Innovation and Entrepreneurship* (1985) and *Managing the Nonprofit Organization* (1990). Drucker identifies three key factors in entrepreneurship:

- A focus on vision and opportunity;

- The creation of a culture of enterprise; and

- The development of a constituency which continues to suggest innovative and entrepreneurial ideas.

Matthew Pike of the Scarman Trust points out that this emphasis on innovation would exclude someone starting up a bog-standard burger bar – arguably even a credit union – from being called a social entrepreneur, no matter how 'successful' they were financially.

4   Run by organisations like the Scarman Trust, Prince's Trust, Age Concern, Earthwatch Europe, Pre-school Learning Alliance, CSV, Northern Ireland Environment Link, Suffolk ACRE, Mind, The Peabody Trust, BTCV, Voluntary Action Cumbria. At the time of writing (November 1999), some 6,000 awards had been handed out, with another 34,000 still to go (Millennium Commission, 1999).

5   You and Yours, Radio 4, February 2001.

6   Johnston & Jowell, 1999.

7   'Us', *The Guardian Weekend*, 8 January 2000.

8   Jonathan Freedland, *Bring Home the Revolution: the case for a British republic,* 4th Estate, London, 1999; 'Us', The Guardian Weekend, 8 January 2000.

9   SPARC tries to avoid specialisation by insisting that all staff pass on 50 percent of their job responsibilities every year. This gifting ritual allows for horizontal learning to take place because generic and well-rounded skills can thus be co-developed.

SPARC maintains its independence by a multiplicity of funding with no more than 15 percent of the organisation's income from one source at any one time. As its name suggests, it works to catalyse grass roots groups to build up a mass membership base and train its trainers to disseminate knowledge and skill horizontally. The two broad based people's organisations that SPARC works closely with are the National Pavement Dwellers Association, which is working on accessing land for self-build housing projects in 21 Indian cities and Mahila Milan, a women's co-operative savings and micro-credit organisation.

For Sheela Patel, the key challenge for voluntary organisations anywhere in the world is to 'create the physical, cultural, social and economic space to facilitate popular reflection.' Creating this space can in a natural way spark mutual action for solutions that local people know but that no professionals ask their views about or give them the freedom to experiment on.

10 Burke, Edmund, *Reflections on the Revolution in France*, Hackett, 1987, p100.

11 The original Greek word for economics, oikonomia, means householding, and emphasised economic self-reliance and local production for local needs. Indeed until 1939, 96 percent of food consumed in Europe was still being grown and provided regionally. Sixty years later, within the regions of the UK, this ratio of self-sufficiency has been turned on its head.

12 Various Department of Trade and Industry reports cited in Conaty & Fisher, New Economics Foundation, 1999.

13 *Poverty, Social Exclusion and Microfinance in Britain*, Rogaly, Fisher and Mayo, Oxfam GB / New Economics Foundation, 1999.

14 The sector is quite dynamic, with around 8–11,000 charities being added each year and 4–7,000 being deleted from the total each year (Pharaoh, 1996 & 1998). In other words, the number of organisations is growing in net terms. This is generally held to be a good thing; an indicator of a vibrant and successful sector (what this growth really says about effectiveness is a different point). There are some 26,000 registered charities in Scotland. Assuming a pro rata number of organisations in Northern Ireland would give 5,000. Of these, not all are operational. Some 45,000 other organisations on the England and Wales charity register appear to have no income; NCVO assumes that these are 'likely to be moribund'. In Scotland, 11 per cent of all charities are said to be 'moribund' (NCVO, 1998). The very term moribund is indicative of the way the formal end of the sector views no-income groups; there must be thousands of social enterprises which currently have no income, and no paid staff, but are far from moribund. A more conservative estimate suggests 120,000 charities.

15 **Narrow & broad dimensions of the voluntary sector**

	Groups covered	**Numbers**
Narrow	Registered charities only, excluding educational establishments & housing associations	200,000–240,000
Broad	Registered charities plus educational establishments, places of worship, housing associations, recreation & business associations	378,000–418,000

Source: Kendall & Knapp in CAF, 1998

16 The ratio is something like 1:1.44. The Scottish CVO is doing pilot studies in Glasgow, Perth and elsewhere on the numbers of unregistered voluntary organisations, which may well revise this estimate upwards.

17 Elsdon *et al., Voluntary Organisations: citizenship, learning and change*, National Institute of Adult Continuing Education, Leicester, 1995.

18 The latter figure ties in well with the recent British Social Attitudes survey which shows that around 10 per cent of the population are a 'truly activist core' (Johnston & Jowell, 1999). To put these numbers in perspective, adding in MSEs makes the voluntary sector three or more times as big as previously thought, in terms of sheer numbers of organisations. In terms of people involved, the formal charities employ 485,000 people, equivalent to 319,000 full time posts. To this, add in the three million part time volunteers who work at the formal charities (equivalent to 1.6 million full time posts). This gives 3.5 million people involved in charities, as opposed to potentially 5 million involved in informal groups.

19 Pete Raynard & Sara Murphy, NEF with ACEVO, 2000.

20 The Home Office's LOVAS project seems to be doing this well, if slowly. The Policy Action Team 9 also had six months to produce a report, and also concentrated most of their 'field work' on two places: Sheffield and Gloucestershire.

21 *Can Do*, leaflet, The Scarman Trust, London, 2000.

22 The forthcoming and eagerly awaited analyses of the 1996 Home Office LOVAS area studies and other initiatives in Scotland should certainly help.

23 The standard classification developed by Johns Hopkins University does not work all that well for the informal, community end of the sector.

24 Thanks to Barry Knight for pointing out to us that these scenarios must remain hypothetical until we or other researchers undertake far larger statistical analysis of the development plans and histories of MSEs.

25 Surveyed in 1996 by the Home Office's LOVAS study (June 1999).

26 Anne-Marie McGeogh, personal communication, December 1999.

27 Personal communication 20 May 1999.

28 Perry Walker *et al., LETS on Low Income*, New Economics Foundation, 1996.

29 'Help with the first steps', Michael Pitchford, in: *Voluntary Voice*, April 1999.

30 Robinson *et al.*, *Social Enterprise Zones,* 1998, page 19.

31 Candy Weston, personal communication about Choices for Bristol, July 1998.

32 Tony Farley, 'Are you doing what you say you're doing?', in: *Voluntary Voice*, December 1999–January 2000.

33 Towards a National Strategy for Neighbourhood Renewal: summary of the report by Policy Action Team 9: Community Self Help, December 1999.